PRESENTING

Avi

Twayne's United States Authors Series
Young Adult Authors

Patricia J. Campbell, General Editor

TUSAS 682

Avi in 1992

Photo courtesy of Gabriel Kahn

PRESENTING

Avi

Susan P. Bloom
Cathryn M. Mercier

Twayne Publishers
An Imprint of Simon & Schuster Macmillan
New York

Prentice Hall International
London Mexico City New Delhi Singapore Sydney Toronto

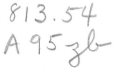

813.54
A95zb

Twayne's United States Authors Series No. 682
Young Adult Authors

Presenting Avi
Susan P. Bloom and Cathryn M. Mercier

Twayne Publishers
An Imprint of Simon & Schuster Macmillan
1633 Broadway
New York, NY 10019

Library of Congress Cataloging-in-Publication Data

Bloom, Susan P.
  Presenting Avi / Susan P. Bloom, Cathryn M. Mercier.
    p. cm.— (Twayne's United States authors series ; TUSAS 682. Young adult authors)
  Includes bibliographical references and index.
  Summary: A critical introduction to the life and work of the prolific writer of young adult and children's books.
  ISBN 0-8057-4569-6
  1. Avi, 1937- —Criticism and interpretation. 2. Young adult fiction, American—History and criticism. 3. Children's stories, American—History and criticism. [1. Avi, 1937- —Criticism and interpretation. 2. American literature—History and criticism.]
I. Mercier, Cathryn M. II. Title. III. Series : Twayne's United States authors series ; TUSAS 682. IV. Series : Twayne's United States authors series. Young adult authors.
  PS3551.V5Z59   1997
  813'.54—dc21   96-53878
                                                                      CIP
                                                                      AC

10 9 8 7 6 5 4 3 2 1

Printed in the United States of America

to the memory of two dear true friends—
Celia Diemont Arovas and Eileen Alperstein
S.P.B.

to the subversive Curt Priest, with love
C.M.M.

Contents

Acknowledgments

We are indebted to Avi for his generosity and support as we worked on this book. In both extended conversations in person and on the telephone, he accommodated all our concerns and responded to all our queries. He generously made available not only photographs of himself and his family, which we have included in this book, but also material from his earliest years as a fledgling writer, as an adolescent journal keeper, and as a frustrated high school student.

We thank Avi's editor, Richard Jackson, for his openness and kindness. Orchard Books itself supplied Avi's books in both galley and hard copy as soon as we requested them.

The moral and financial support of the Simmons College Fund for Research provided us with additional encouragement to pursue this project.

Patty Campbell's positive and thoughtful feedback on our manuscript and her directed comments and questions gave considerable shape to the final product; for this we are particularly appreciative.

Finally, we gratefully acknowledge permission to use the following:

Unpublished correspondence between Avi and Richard Jackson.
Unpublished conversation between Avi and Richard Jackson at "A Room of One's Own" Summer Symposium in Children's Literature at the Center for the Study of Children's Literature, Simmons College, Boston, in July 1995, used with permission of Avi and Richard Jackson.
All photographs used are published with the kind permission of Avi.

Selected quotations from "We" by Richard Jackson, published in *The Horn Book Magazine*, May/June 1993.

All otherwise uncredited quotations are from interviews with Avi by the authors, October 1995 and July 1996.

Preface

We first met Avi in 1987 when he proposed and then taught a graduate course at the Simmons College Center for the Study of Children's Literature in Boston. The course, which Avi originally titled "Aesthetics and Ideology in Children's Literature," articulated and acted on Avi's belief in the necessity of reading and reviewing books not in isolation but within the larger context of the author's body of work. For study, Avi selected four popular writers and required that students read, or reread specifically for this course, the authors' complete works along with supplementary readings in literary criticism. His course syllabus states the seminar's focus on "the writer's development, form and content, literary achievement, stated and unstated ideology" (unpublished syllabus, 1987). Such intensive attention to an author works to frame individual titles within the whole opus, allowing readers to make connections between books.

This approach to an author's work forms a response to Avi's dissatisfaction with the way in which the review media too often appraise children's and young adult literature, especially his own books. In a *School Library Journal* article titled "Reviewing the Reviewers," published in March of 1986, when Avi practiced as a librarian at Trenton State College and had already published 17 books, Avi asks: "Is it not possible for the profession to have, *as a matter of course*, critical surveys of an author's work, critical essays (not just bibliographies) that cover genre, subject, regions, problems, and so forth?" (115). Further, he states that "a person who accepts the responsibility of passing critical judgment should not only accept the need for some knowledge of the field (past and present but also the body of work of a given author . . . [and] that reviewers take upon themselves knowledge of an author's work and respond to us as writers, not as brandnames" (115). The course Avi designed and brought to Simmons meets these demands.

Whereas reviews written for a purchasing audience of librarians, booksellers, parents, and teachers, among others, may not always be able to address the author specifically, a course can—and Avi designed his course so that it would. In the model Avi developed, students followed their immersion in an author's work with the rare opportunity to meet with that author in a small, intimate group for three hours. Here, students-as-critics employed their well-informed, well-prepared understanding of the author's canon to respond directly to the author. To our delight, not only did the course prove successful and popular with students, but Avi also reported having fellow authors call him, asking to be studied in this thorough and serious manner. Indeed, at least one author rejoiced in learning something new about herself as expressed in her writing from this careful, thoughtful group of readers.

The very year Avi stopped teaching the course and Susan Bloom assumed its responsibilities, Avi became one of its first subjects. His enthusiastic response to this scrutiny revealed that he gained insight into his own work, adding personal validity to his initial justification for this kind of critical exploration.

It seems only fitting to broaden this methodology into a book-length study of Avi. Since his work at Simmons, his popularity with young readers continues to soar. His recognition by the world of adult critics appears to be catching up. While Avi's books tended to be reviewed in significant professional journals, that attention grew and took on fresh seriousness with *The Fighting Ground. The True Confessions of Charlotte Doyle*, another award-winning book, marked additional forward movement in both Avi's popularity and critical acclaim.

This biocritical study serves as a paradoxical opportunity to step out of the stream of Avi's prolific writings, even as we step deeply into those waters. As we view the individual titles within the context of all his books and as we consider all the books within the context of each book, we cannot help but notice emerging "aesthetics and ideology," recurring patterns and themes, and the interweaving of Avi's life into his fiction. In that early syllabus proposal, Avi reminded his students of something we became increasingly aware of as we ventured toward making sense of the complexities of his work: "The study of fiction is not a branch of cryptanalysis. Fiction does not 'mean.' Fiction is a written art in which experience is manipulated (consciously or unconsciously) into forms which represent life. Personal judgment based on your own experience is the place where all responses to literature are made." This book, like Avi's course, attempts to go beyond personal likes and dislikes by informing one's reading experience with critical interpretation.

Ultimately, interpretation remains all that we can offer. Our topics and organization, our selection of specific books, themes, and characters are peculiarly ours. While we identify ideas that appear throughout Avi's fiction, we also recognize that each book could be considered under another—usually under many other— thematic headings. *Beyond the Western Sea. Book One: The Escape from Home* proves as much a novel about truthtelling and masquerade, about risk taking and magic, about history and subversion, about storytelling and style as it is about Avi's artistic conception of family. More than anything else, Avi's intertextuality in his own books—their references and allusions to and interaction with others of his books—shows itself again and again. The vessel *Seahawk* surfaces in *The Man Who Was Poe*, *The True Confessions of Charlotte Doyle*, and *Beyond the Western Sea*. Why does the address 84 Benefit Street keep reappearing? Images of sailing, herons, historical settings, and geographical locations reoccur, much to the delighted satisfaction of the discovering reader.

One element stands as a key to reading Avi—recognition of the sheer quantity of knowledge and insight he commands about literature for children and young adults. He trained as a librarian, practices as a teacher of children's and young adult literature for children and adults, writes critical and reflective essays as well as novels, and continues his work as historiographer—researching, writing, and rewriting history, including the history of children's literature. Perhaps it is these many aspects of Avi that combine to form a writer whom critics consistently assess as always experimental and versatile. Avi himself may reject this evaluation, given his commitment to the omnipresence of a good, strong story in fiction and his awareness of intertextualities and repeating patterns in his oeuvre. Certainly, Avi does bring to fiction for children and young adults a vision of its potential for vitality and excitement. In a letter to the editor in the May/June 1990 *Horn Book Magazine,* Avi defines his view of good writing and good writers for children:

> My son Kevin had a great love of the novels of Edith Nesbit, of the *Treasure Seekers* brood and Oswald in particular. One evening at the end of our bedtime reading, Kevin (he was nine or ten) snuggled into his pillow as he asked me if he could write to Nesbit and tell her how much he liked her books.
> "That's a great idea," I said, "but I'm afraid it's not possible. She died a long, long time ago."
> "Died?" cried Kevin, sitting bolt upright in his bed. He had a truly bewildered look on his face. "Before I was born?"
> "Yes."
> "But then—how does she know so much about *me*?"
> His words have become my notion of what a great writer for kids is all about. (261)

This book can only begin to explore the multifaceted ways in which Avi knows his readers.

Chronology

1937   Avi Wortis born 23 December in New York City.

1942   Attends Public School #8 [Robert Fulton School] in Brooklyn, New York.

1951   Enters Stuyvesant High School, which he attends for one quarter.

1955   Graduates from Elizabeth Irwin High School in New York City, setting for *S.O.R. Losers*.

Attends Antioch College.

1959   Receives a Bachelor of Arts in history from the University of Wisconsin in Madison.

1962   Earns a Master of Arts in drama at the University of Wisconsin.

1963   Marries Joan Gainer, a weaver.

1964   Earns his MLS in library science at Columbia University.

1966   Son Shaun born.

1968   Second son Kevin born.

1970   Takes a job as librarian at Trenton State College following his move to New Jersey.

First published work, *Things That Sometimes Happen*.

1972   *Snail Tale: The Adventures of a Rather Small Snail*.

1975   *No More Magic.*

1977   Publishes first historical fiction, *Captain Grey.*

1978   First parody of nineteenth-century melodrama, *Emily Upham's Revenge; or, How Deadwood Dick Saved the Banker's Niece.*

1979   *Night Journeys.*

1980   *Encounter at Easton,* sequel to *Night Journeys.*

        Man from the Sky.

        History of Helpless Harry: To Which Is Added a Variety of Amusing and Entertaining Adventures.

1981   *A Place Called Ugly.*

        Who Stole the Wizard of Oz?

1982   Divorces Joan Gainer.

        Sometimes I Think I Hear My Name.

1983   Marries Coppelia Kahn, professor of English.

        Shadrach's Crossing.

1984   *S.O.R. Losers.*

        Devil's Race.

1985   *Bright Shadow.*

1986   *Wolf Rider: A Tale of Terror.*

1987   Takes up residence in Providence home, which is setting for *Something Upstairs.*

        Devil's Race.

1988   *Something Upstairs: A Tale of Ghosts.*

        Romeo and Juliet—Together (and Alive!) at Last, sequel to *S.O.R. Losers.*

1. Avi as Storyteller

The story is primitive, it reaches back to the origins of literature, before reading was discovered, and it appeals to what is
primitive in us.

—E. M. Forster[1]

Where and how does an author learn the craft of telling stories?
Avi's experience reaches far back into his family history. Avi
traces professional storytellers in his family to his paternal great-
grandfather, Eliakim Zunser (1836–1913). Nicknamed Yakum, he
served as a *badchen*, the Yiddish term for a folk bard, at Jewish
weddings. His job as merrymaker was to make people laugh and
cry at the wedding. He would begin by talking seriously about the
bride and the groom. Continuing his story, Yakum extemporized
in song and poetry and grew increasingly madcap as he entertained and celebrated with the wedding guests. Eliakum Zunser's
son Charles, Avi's maternal grandfather, later established his
own reputation as a storyteller. Avi recalls this grandfather as a
captivating teller of tales, so effective at the emotive drama of
telling stories that the young Avi laughed at punchlines delivered
in Yiddish even though he did not understand them.[2] Taking his
storytelling to the printed page, Avi's maternal great-grandfather, Shomer, wrote romance novels about poor Jewish girls who
fall in love and marry wealthy men. His fame rests largely on his
censure by Shalom Aleichem for debasing Jewish culture and language (Waldman).

According to Avi, his "family has a long writing tradition. One
great-grandfather was a poet, another a novelist and dramatist.

1

Avi's paternal grandparents Wortis (front) and his great-uncle.

My grandmother was a playwright. Both my parents aspired to be writers, too, and published extensively in history and the sciences. My twin sister Emily Leider is both a poet and literary critic."[3] "That my twin sister is also a writer says much about the world I grew up in. For I come from a family and a house full of books. Strange if we hadn't become writers."[4] Avi reports that his

Joseph and Helen Wortis, Avi's parents, in 1959.

Avi's childhood family about 1940 (from left to right: Avi's aunts, Beadie (top) and Rosellen; Beadie's son Alan; Avi's grandmother and grandfather; Avi's brother, Henry; Avi; Avi's father, Joseph; and Avi's sister Emily.

Avi at Long Beach in the summer of 1943.

mother read to him every night; independently he read widely across genres including classic literature for children and adults, contemporary children's books, adult books, and, "not the least, comic books."[5]

Growing up in a brownstone in Brooklyn Heights, New York, Avi lived around the corner from an aunt and cousins.[6] His cousin Michael constituted Avi's first audience. Together they also read comic books and listened to the radio. For Avi, storytelling

Avi in 1957 in his parents' home.

became play, and play involved telling stories. "Watching, listening, reading: the natural education of a writer" (*Speaking*, 13).

Things That Sometimes Happen

That type of game-playing took on new life when Avi raised his two sons. "My oldest would tell me what the story should be about—he would invent stuff, a story about a glass of water and so forth."[7] This father-son activity evolved into Avi's first book for children, entitled *Things That Sometimes Happen*. The subtitle, "very short stories for very young readers," aptly describes the 30 illustrated pieces in this 78-page collection. The stories feature a series of prototypical characters: the Little Boy, the Black Crayon, Mama, the Stars, a Kite, the Ice Cream Cone, the Little Girl. The anonymity of the characters enables young readers to identify with them quickly; however, story, the most basic element of all fiction, drives this collection. In the book's final piece, entitled "A Story about a Story," Avi constructs an eloquent description of story as having "lots of interesting things to say, even funny things. It went on, and on, with all sorts of things happening"[8] requiring an ending.

The individual stories run anywhere from a half-page to four pages in length. They center on an ordinary event, although a dreamlike quality often transforms that ordinary occurrence into an extraordinary one. For example, a little boy walking in the park soon finds himself in the jungle, where he discovers an enormous green mushroom. The title story introduces the conjunction of the child's here-and-now and the fantastic world of her imagination. Though preceding it by some fifteen years, this book reminds one of Maira Kalman's *Hey Willy, See the Pyramids* (Viking, 1988). While Kalman captures a child's view of the world—often perceived of as simple, illogical, and downright zany to the adults—in illustrations and narrative viewpoint, Avi succeeds by relating a child-like series of events as story. "They sound like a first grader's first story efforts, but they are not as spontaneous and show the control of an adult writer. . . . " (note 9) Avi manifests that control in his recognition of the simultaneity of the routine and the hyperbolic in the child's world.

This book seems at home in today's pop culture. Although one critic in 1970 reviewed the book saying that "the same thing happens: nothing,"[9] viewers of the popular television comedy "Seinfeld" embrace and construct shows about nothing. Clearly, *nothing* does not mean nothing in this context; rather, it points to a celebration of the ordinary. Similarly, Avi's final "Story about a Story" now earns critical attention as metafictional play and can take company with other popular books such as *The Stinky Cheese Man and Other Fairly Stupid Tales* (Jon Scieszka and Lane Smith, 1992), David Macaulay's *Black and White* (1990; the 1991 Caldecott winner) and his recent publication *Short Cuts* (1995), and Chris Van Allsburg's *Bad Day at Riverbend* (1995).

Snail Tale

Whereas *Things That Sometimes Happen* presents short, independent stories, Avi's next book, *Snail Tale: The Adventures of a Rather Small Snail,* relates a single, circular story. From its opening statement to its appendix, this work demonstrates the author's self-consciousness about storytelling. The book begins by treating ways in which storytellers learn their trade. "Avon, a rather small snail, read a book every day. He loved to read because books told him all about the things that creatures did when they went on adventures."[10] To Avi, then, adventures build stories.

This chapter book for newly independent readers adopts the traditional home-journey-home pattern. Avon and his guide—the seasoned ant adventurer Edward—set out in search of adventures that will ensure a happy life. The bookish Avon listens carefully to the Newt's wisdom: "Remember, lad, . . . if it's going to be tomorrow, it might as well be today. And if it's today, it could have been yesterday. If it *was* yesterday, then you're over and done with it, and can write your own book" (*Snail,* 6). Aspiring to be a writer, Avon cannot ignore these words and prepares for immediate departure. This call to adventure stems from Avon's desire to participate more fully, as both creator and reader, in the world of traditional literature. Avon and Edward embark on their journey only to travel unwittingly in a circle; their place of departure becomes their point of arrival.

The Newt asks for a report of Avon's most exciting experience and hears an eventful, animated story of an escapade that never actually happened. In recounting the tales of his trip, Avon discovers that the greatest adventure is storytelling itself. This recognition yields his insightful comment that "to go on a long trip, to come so far from where you live, then to come across a magic castle that has all the comforts of home" brings happiness. Not only does Avon journey away from physical home only to return to it ultimately, but he also travels metaphorically between the roles of reader and teller. Avon begins and ends as a reader; the adventures show him the source of story, which enables him to return to the familiar home of reading with the knowledgeable appreciation of a storyteller. The perceptive Edward realizes the significance of the change in Avon. After the "Frog Adventure Appendix" (*Snail*, 47), Avon

> . . . whispered to Edward, "That was so interesting, I wish it had happened."
> "I don't think so," suggested Edward, wisely. "The best stories are heard, not seen."
> Avon nodded thoughtfully, picked up a book, and began to listen. (*Snail*, 47–48)

Like *Things That Sometimes Happen*, *Snail Tale* reveals a metafictional self-consciousness. One reviewer considered this book to be a series of disjointed, never-fully-realized fantasies because the "small creatures along the way [of Avon's adventures] fail to provide . . . opportunities for real heroism."[11] Margery Fisher (1976), however, understood the book's reach much better:

> You can if you wish read [*Snail Tale*] as a light-hearted satire on the way a writer manipulates reality. Avon's reverential belief in the infallibility of traditional literature is seen to be relevant to this approach. Hearing a sound of woe in the distance, he announces "I think we should stop . . . That's what they do in the books."[12]

In its purest form, then, *Snail Tale* acts as a story about telling stories.

The Bird, the Frog, and the Light

Although *The Bird, the Frog, and the Light* was not published until 1994, Avi completed the manuscript for this work early in his writing life. This fable harkens back to his earlier works in its concern with reading and storytelling. The self-appointed frog king learns humility when a bird brings the light of reading into his dark, illiterate life. Opening as a traditional once-upon-a-time tale, this picture book travels a circular path. With light as the defining metaphor, the fable shifts from under- to above- to underground again and parallels the temporal framework of the story, which moves from morning through night to dawn. The frog beckons the bird to bring a ray of sun into his kingdom because he is "tired of feeling [his] magnificence . . . [he] must see it all."[13] The light exposes the true paucity of his domain, and learning to read illuminates it.

The Man from the Sky

Reading takes on new importance in *The Man from the Sky*. Dysgraphic himself, Avi calls it his book about dyslexia. As one of the "Capers for Every Kid" series that uses short chapters, large type against ample white space, and generous illustrations, even the book's presentation suggests potential mastery to the challenged reader. Avi chooses to tell the single story of a boy coming to grips with his disability in two convergent strands. In the first, 11-year-old Jamie Peters spends the month of August with his grandparents. Each day he looks at the sky to "read the clouds." There he envisions the dragons, ladies, and knights that become the stuff of his storytelling. The second story line follows Ed Goddard, a former parachutist, and his plans to steal a million dollars from a plane in flight. When Jamie's sky-watching makes him witness to the thief's fall from the air, the stories merge.

Gillian, a neighborhood girl, envies Jamie's capacity to tell stories from watching the sky. Still, she does not believe Jamie's fantastic tale about the man who fell from the sky—until she finds a satchel filled with cash. When Goddard takes her hostage, Jamie first must convince others of Gillian's danger and then decipher the messages about Goddard's intended destination that Gillian scratches in the dirt.

Avi celebrates reading in this novel in part because Jamie succeeds in decoding Gillian's message and ultimately because Gillian shares with Jamie her cloud-visions of the alphabet, the components of all stories told, written, and read. Again, Avi's characters revel in storytelling itself and learn the craft of narration. Because Avi credits even the struggling reader with the intelligence to sustain two engaging story lines, the "real strength of this book is the alternating chapters telling first Goddard's and then Jamie's story in uncluttered prose."[14] He motivates, then rewards, the reader.

Who Stole the Wizard of Oz?

Another Caper title, *Who Stole the Wizard of Oz?*, continues to offer a dynamic story in an approachable format. Here, too, Avi's story develops as a mystery; however, the solution to this tale relies on experienced, avaricious readers. Avi wrote this book when he worked as a librarian and teacher of children's literature. In it, he uses the library as setting and again establishes reading as empowering. The intertextual references to the well-known children's books *Treasure Island, Winnie-the-Pooh, The Wonderful Wizard of Oz, The Wind in the Willows, Alice's Adventures in Wonderland,* and *Through the Looking Glass* provide subtle clues to the location of a hidden treasure even as they note the serious artistry and influence of classic children's literature.

Ultimately, everything in *Who Stole the Wizard of Oz?* returns to a celebration of reading. Although the dreaded Miss McPhearson, a sixth-grade teacher, warns "no mysteries, no make-believe, no romantic adventure. . . . Children your age are beyond such nonsense,"[15] the novel unravels as a mystery in which the ability to make-believe, to imagine beyond oneself, and the courage to undertake a romantic adventure combine with the capacity to see the logic in nonsense. Becky and Toby Almano, the first appearance of twins in Avi's books, are searching for missing children's books donated to the town library's book sale. They quickly identify the common qualities of these books and follow the maps they provide. Not only do the children find out who stole *The Wizard of Oz* but they also learn why. "Avi does keep readers puzzling and piecing out the solution"[16] as the twins read and talk about their reading.

Romeo and Juliet—Together

Avi's clever incorporation of intertextual references continues in *Romeo and Juliet—Together (and Alive!) at Last*. In addition, this book extends the use of dialogue as a storytelling mechanism well beyond the plot-revealing conversations held by Becky and Toby. Avi's use of dialogue here anticipates its use to both unify elements of the novel and advance story in *Who Was That Masked Man, Anyhow?* As in theater, dialogue advances plot, reveals character, and tells a story. Early in the novel, an exchange between the main characters, Ed Sitrow (with characteristic mischief, Avi used his last name spelled in reverse) and his best friend Pete Saltz (Avi's best friend from childhood was named Saltz), demonstrates an awareness of the connection between speaking about story and story itself:

> "You *did* set me up, Sitrow, admit it."
> "Well . . ."
> "Yes or no?"
> "I thought we were best friends."
> "Aren't we?"
> He looked at me, steely-eyed. "Let's see what happens."[17]

As in theater, dialogue largely reveals what happens throughout the next 21 short chapters.

"When Shakespeare penned the line 'a poor player that struts and frets his hour upon the stage,' he surely couldn't know to what lengths the strutting and fretting would be carried in this imaginative, cleverly written, laugh-out-loud story centered on one of the Bard's creations."[18] The playwright Avi stages all elements of this return to South Orange River School into a winning comedy, despite the tragic intentions of Shakespeare's work.

The central plot element in *Romeo and Juliet—Together* revolves around Sitrow's desire to help his friend Saltz, whom he perceives to be in love. Before he can assist, he must first know what love is himself, and he must turn to the dictionary rather than to experience.

Putting "Romeo and Juliet" in the hands of untrained, unsupervised eighth graders with a compelling interest in matchmaking naturally results in a variety of botched lines. Avi demonstrates his facility with wordplay in earlier texts. However, given the interdependence of dialogue and story in this novel, he engages here in more sophisticated punning. For example, the group's playbill lists these characters: Ben Volvo, Bath Asar, and Fryer Laurence (*Romeo*, 78). Just as the play gets under way, the nervous Romeo asks "Is she a catapult?" (*Romeo*, 87); in the penultimate scene, Juliet dies, and the mournful nurse cries, "She's dead, deceased; she's dead, I lack a day" (*Romeo*, 112). Of course, only readers acquainted with the original play will recognize these lines as bungled; only the experienced reader will grasp the intertextual jokes.

The last action in the novel shows Sitrow reading "Anthony and Cleopatra" and judging it not "half bad" (*Romeo*, 122). An early diary of Avi's contains an entry reporting his first reading of Plato at a very young age as "not bad." The resonant intertextual references in Avi's fiction continually assert the author's attribution of his readers with intelligence, knowledge, and the potential to appreciate literature.

The character of Annabelle Stackpole (also known as Juliet) reminds one of Snail: she continually buries her nose in books. However, Annabelle's reading diet consists largely of romantic fiction. Avi comments on this tendency both openly and slyly. Pitting the tragedy of forbidden true love in Romeo and Juliet against the melodramas in Annabelle's popular fiction, he remarks—by Sitrow's asking Annabelle if her book won a Newbery Award— about the fluff of her reading material. Here, too, Avi broadens the malapropisms beyond dialogue and into commentary about reading.

Wolf Rider

Dialogue takes on increased narrative significance in *Wolf Rider: A Tale of Terror*. The novel opens with a chilling telephone conversation between 15-year-old Andy Zadinski and Zeke, a confessing, would-be murderer. This disturbing exchange closely replicates an actual telephone conversation in Avi's life. While living in New Jersey, Avi received a random anonymous call from someone who claimed to have murdered a woman. Although Avi acted responsibly, keeping the caller on the line while the police attempted to trace the call's origin, Avi was advised to dismiss the episode from his mind—"he had done all he could."[19] Like Andy, Avi could not so easily forget the terror or the possibility that someone's life might be in jeopardy. Should he persist in attempting to reach the alleged intended victim, the police cautioned Avi, he might be assumed guilty himself. Avi purged himself of this haunting event by transforming it into a novel whose "charged beginning electrifies a plot that sizzles with suspense every inch of the way. Avi fortifies this excitement with staccato dialogue . . ." (Elleman 1986, 505). Three strands of dialogue propel the story as Zeke's confession disturbs Andy enough for him to seek resolution. Andy turns to his father for counsel; then he looks for Nina Klemmer, the college student Zeke intends to kill; and, finally, Andy decides to discover Zeke's real identity. In Andy's search for the truth, each conversation simultaneously reveals and conceals.

Initial conversations between Andy and his father appear unguarded and genuine on both sides. Andy must tell someone about the disturbing telephone call and trustingly turns to his father, Dr. Zadinski, who listens carefully to his son. However, by the conversation's end, Dr. Zadinski dismisses the call as crank and advises Andy to "forget about the whole thing."[20] Communication between the two continues to break down with each subsequent discussion, and Andy's trust in his father begins to dissolve. Believing in the authenticity of the call—and in its promised danger—Andy cannot and will not forget about it. After involving others in the situation, Andy continually returns to his father for affirmation. His confidence in his father erodes more each time Dr. Zadinski states his disbelief and as his impatience with Andy's obsession grows. Their early quiet, controlled discussions gradually disintegrate into yelling matches that pit father against son. Ultimately, communication ceases when Dr. Zadinski accuses his son of placing the call, then labels his son "a very mixed up young man" (*Wolf*, 105) who is "nuts" (*Wolf*, 105). No longer believing in his son yet unsure about the kind of help Andy needs, Dr. Zadinski eliminates all possible exchanges between the two when he determines to send Andy away.

The more his father questions him, the more Andy assumes responsibility for preventing any harm resulting from the telephone call. Andy turns to the police; however, like his father, this authority also refuses involvement and casts suspicion onto the well-meaning Andy. Hoping to warn the intended victim, Andy locates Nina Klemmer, who immediately refuses to listen to him. Nina quickly and viciously questions Andy's sanity. Fear may prohibit her from hearing, but her complete misunderstanding of Andy's motivations results in his victimization. She casts him as villain and reports him to the police, and he becomes labeled as the very stalker from whom he seeks to protect her.

Rejected and frustrated, Andy turns to the only one who will believe him: Zeke. Andy conducts a comprehensive telephone campaign that results in his voice identification of Zeke as Philip Lucas, an honored math professor and colleague of his father. Soon, Lucas launches his own telephone search to identify the voice to whom he confessed, the voice that now could destroy him. The parallel investigations amplify the novel's tension as Andy and Lucas move closer to meeting. In Andy's desperation to save his honor, he mistakenly assumes that "he knew who Zeke was, but Lucas knew nothing of him. From perfect safety—by phone—he could pressure Lucas" (*Wolf*, 115). Just as Andy strips away Zeke's anonymity, so does Lucas work to discover Andy.

Andy makes one final attempt to contact the adults on whom he should be able to rely. Tension accelerates again as each attempt fails and Andy is driven to meet Lucas, the only one who can restore his honor as a truthteller. Although Avi controls the reader's knowledge of most characters through their dialogue, the narrative point of view becomes increasingly dual as Andy and Lucas move closer to meeting. Lucas emerges from the anonymity of a telephone voice as Andy becomes more certain about Zeke's true identity. Avi then slowly starts to reveal to the reader Lucas's perspective. Still, even as readers witness Lucas's wiles in constructing an alibi as he plans to meet Andy, even as readers feel the genuine threat Lucas poses to Andy, Lucas's motivations remain unclear. Does he intend to kill Nina? Why did he make the telephone call?

Until the fatal interaction between Lucas and Andy, however, Andy's motivations have been relatively apparent: He initially wanted to save Nina because, after his mother's accidental death, "to Andy, talk of death was never—ever—a joke" (*Wolf*, 28). Even as the novel nears its end, that motivation remains intact. As he rides with Lucas

> Andy felt as though his chest was full of stones. "I . . . don't want," Andy stammered, "don't want . . . to be killed. . . . I don't want people to die . . . ever. . . . Just to live." (*Wolf*, 188)

Avi shifts Andy's motivation with remarkable subtlety. Each occasion of disbelief overlays Andy's original motivation with the more essential need to prove himself trustworthy. That motivation, too, alters as fear for his own life increases. Andy's final action, his unspoken witnessing of Lucas's death, yields the silence his father so desired. His motivation here rests on his epiphany that knowledge of "what had happened . . . would kill his father and Andy knew how much he needed him and loved him" (*Wolf*, 202). In the end, Andy's quiescence hides the very

trustworthiness he so wanted to prove. In so doing, Avi questions
the nature of a relationship in which life, need, and love rest on a
foundation of deception.

Dr. Zadinski mourns even as he accepts the duplicity necessary
to maintain a relationship with his son. In disposing of Lucas's
cufflink, which he discovered in Andy's closet, he throws out the
honesty that originally characterized their relationship. He views
Andy now as "an entirely new person, a stranger" (*Wolf*, 198).
Unsure of what actually happened between Andy and Lucas yet
unwilling to know the truth, Dr. Zadinski allows fear to silence
him in relation to his son.

Responses to this ending vary from "an ironically structured
conclusion [in which Andy and his father] recognize the depth of
their mutual feelings while unnecessarily attempting to protect
each other" (Elleman, 1986, 506) to "a disturbing, ambiguous
parting of father and son."[21] Avi's use of dialogue both to mask
and to reveal complement his dual stories of "a conventional mystery with all the threads tied neatly at the end"[22] and a "psychological study" (Vose, 111–12), to result in "a gripping and above-
average YA thriller" (Hearne, 61). Perhaps the most chilling
element arises when the conversations that dominate this narrative all culminate in silence, all end in promises not to tell.

Poppy

Poppy combines the simplicity of an animal adventure like *Snail
Tale* with the dynamic telling of *Wolf Rider* into a "good old-fashioned *story* with an exciting plot, well-drawn characters, and a
satisfying ending. . . ."[23] Avi's creation of Dimwood Forest and
the winning anthropomorphic creatures echoes his childhood
favorite, *The Wind in the Willows*. Like Kenneth Grahame, Avi
starts his mouse character Poppy out as a homebody. Timid and
respectful, Poppy is a follower; by novel's end, however, she
emerges as a confident and admired leader. She journeys away
from home only to return there again. Discovery of a new, more
hospitable home proves an important boon to her travels.

As does Robert C. O'Brien in *Mrs. Frisby and the Rats of NIMH*, Avi establishes a realistic terrain on which to set this animal fantasy. The opening map helps orient readers, but one's understanding of this land comes from the details Avi chooses to include. Unlike the other titles discussed in this chapter, *Poppy* opens with a description of the setting.

> A thin crescent moon, high in the sky, shed faint white light over Dimwood Forest. Stars glowed. Breezes full of ripe summer fragrance floated over nearby meadow and hill. Dimwood itself, veiled in darkness, lay utterly still.
> At the very edge of this forest stood an old charred oak on which sat a great horned owl. The owl's name was Mr. Ocax, and he looked like death himself.[24]

The opening map and the first paragraph of the novel establish a panoramic view of the forest. Avi then narrows the scene with a particularity of description that sharply focuses the reader. The specificity of the charred oak heightens the generalized immensity of sky and forest while simultaneously initiating the story with the introduction of a central character.

Here, too, detail plays a defining role. Avi moves from the whole forest to accent Mr. Ocax, who stands guard at the edge of the forest. As an outsider, the owl immediately poses a threat, and soon readers know that Mr. Ocax not only looks like death but also acts like death in not discriminating between victims.

The same pattern serves to introduce the story's hero as well as its nemesis. However, having entered the realm of character, Avi stays there. Mr. Ocax's prowling gaze scans the vista before reaching its ultimate fix.

> He looked at Glitter Creek, home to the fish he found so appetizing; the Tar Road, across which tasty rabbits were known to hop; Jayswood, where meaty chipmunks sometimes skittered before dawn. By swiveling his head he searched the Marsh for a savory frog, then New Field, where, usually, he could count on a delicious vole or two. He looked at Gray House, where Farmer Lamout used to live, then upon the Old Orchard. He even looked, nervously, toward New House. But nowhere did he see a

thing to eat. Profoundly annoyed, Mr. Ocax was beginning to think he would have no dinner that night.

But finally, there—near the top of Bannock Hill, where the ponderosa pines had all been cut, where only a few struggling saplings and bushes grew—he saw movement. Just the glimmer of food was enough to cause his owl's heart to point, his curved black beak to clack, his feathered horns to stand up tall.

Mr. Ocax shifted his head from right to left, forward and back. When he did so, he beheld . . . two mice! Of all the creatures the owl hunted, he enjoyed mice the most. They were the best eating, to be sure, but better still, they were the most fearful, and Mr. Ocax found deep satisfaction in having others afraid of him. And here, after a wait of nearly the whole night, were two savory subjects to terrify before he ate them. (*Poppy*, 1–2)

In addition to providing the information necessary to navigate the adventure's route, this passage fully describes Mr. Ocax's character. Readers immediately discern his devious nature and know not to trust him. At the outset, readers align themselves with Mr. Ocax's yet-to-be-introduced innocent victims.

Describing Mr. Ocax from an omniscient narrator's point of view directs readers' sympathy even before the introduction of other characters, establishing an "us and them" reading of the book— and Mr. Ocax is clearly not wanted among "us." Avi presents the mice not through an all-knowing, directed description but through discourse. Such use of dialogue suggests a relatively unbiased perspective in that it allows readers to judge characters based on what they say and do. One need only follow the conversations between Ragweed and Poppy for a short time to glean the aspects of plot and character that will direct the novel. Slang peppers Ragweed's ungrammatical, hip language, whereas structure and control typify Poppy's. Similarly, their exchanges reveal Ragweed's brazen fearlessness and Poppy's conservative apprehension.

In the first chapter, Mr. Ocax kills Ragweed. Because the nonconforming mouse who has already won the reader's affection no longer figures in the novel, this action provides a daring twist. A less skilled novelist would hardly challenge the reader's expectations. Who will champion the novel? What hero will emerge? The only strong character left is Mr. Ocax, and surely he would be a dastardly hero. And the fainthearted Poppy, who "vow[s] she'll never leave home again" (*Poppy*, 14), is hardly hero material. Yet the title and the courage she musters for the journey homeward foreshadow Poppy's fortitude.

"Older children may recognize the politics of power played out through the three figures who initially dominate Poppy: Mr. Ocax, who cleverly coaxes, rules by fear, and despises those he oppresses; Poppy's father, who threatens dire consequences because he is fearful but has little substance behind his bluster; and Ragweed, who belittles Poppy for her cautious ways, choosing to deny fear entirely and consequently dying in chapter 1" (Phelan, 402). From her father, leader of the field mice, to Mr. Ocax and the most feared porcupines, Poppy faces numerous obstacles. Driven by the need to redeem her honor and her good name and compelled by the desire to remove the community's assessment of her guilt in Ragweed's death, Poppy accepts the call to adventure.

In form true to other classic heroes, Poppy happens upon a guide to her exploits. Entering a log to escape a fox, she disturbs the terrifying porcupine's hibernation and feels doomed. However, Erethizon Dorsatum, the porcupine, surprisingly poses no threat and emerges as Poppy's guide to a new home for the exuberant mouse population. In many ways, Erethizon Dorsatum recalls the robust character of Ragweed: He, too, tells the truth; crass colloquialisms and puns enliven his language, and he acts fearlessly. The first to recognize Poppy's potential, he observes that she is "pretty small to be a heroine" (*Poppy*, 102). He helps Poppy find New House and to expose the false threat Mr. Ocax finds there; more importantly, however, the porcupine teaches Poppy perspective.

Avi develops the character of Erethizon Dorsatum as a complex one. Although the porcupine helps Poppy and seems genuinely to like her, he bargains with her before agreeing to lead her through the forest. New House holds a treasure for him—a salt lick. But, because the salt lick sits high upon a pole, the porcupine cannot reach it. In her desire to discover a new home, Poppy agrees to get the salt lick for him. At this point in the novel, Poppy's promise appears to be a foolhardy one—if a porcupine cannot climb the pole to carry down the salt block, how can a field mouse accomplish the task? Yet, Poppy's determination and her success thus far bolster her self-confidence: She will not break her promise. The impossible job and Poppy's will to complete it create a tension that propels the plot.

The porcupine leads Poppy to New House, to the salt lick, and then he leaves. Poppy trips over one of his quills. Rather than throwing it out, she examines it and realizes its potential. The quill assumes metaphoric significance as it signals Poppy's transition from simply reacting to acting in anticipation of events. She considers the quill and has "an idea. Grasping it by its blunt end, she swished it about a few times. It moved nicely. Like a sword" (*Poppy*, 114). Through the power of her imagination, Poppy transforms the quill into a sword, allowing her symbolically to retain the confidence and protection of her guide, Erethizon Dorsatum. The quill ultimately serves as a weapon in her combat against Mr. Ocax, a battle from which she emerges triumphant.

Poppy's growing reliance on her reason and intelligence prove essential in recognizing the true enemy at New House. Because she thinks about the owl she sees standing guard at New House and compares it to the owls she has known, she recognizes it as an empty threat, a stuffed owl posing no real danger. In fact, Poppy masters Mr. Ocax in two ways: After outsmarting him, she defeats him in battle.

The porcupine gives Poppy confidence, and his quill embodies the courage she now possesses. From him, she also learns how to laugh at herself and her situation. By the novel's end, Poppy not only regards herself more honestly but also sees through the facades of others, especially that of Mr. Ocax: "He's just a frightened bully! she said to herself with jubilation. She had to slap a paw over her mouth to keep from laughing out loud. What fun it would be to humiliate him. Just the idea of it brought a feeling of power" (*Poppy*, 126). As Poppy entertains the thought of humbling her defeated adversary, she shows the barb on her quills.

Taunting the owl and causing him additional pain would cheapen her victory. Because she understands and commands her power, Poppy chooses not to betray the best in herself.

At the novel's opening, the forest only frightens Poppy. She finds it a threatening, gloomy place. Yet, by novel's end, she "absorb[s] the lush view, the way moonlight filtered through the fragrant air, a very tall tree, a particularly beautiful fern, a bush laden with blackberries as big as her head" (*Poppy*, 140). Poppy's survival promotes her recognition of beauty. The Poppy who was frightened by Mr. Ocax now sees such magnificence in his single feather that she takes it with her. Poppy beholds her world anew, a change that accents the completion of her heroic journey. Not only does she return home, but also she arrives carrying the boon of appreciating home.

Poppy adds Mr. Ocax's feather to the sash that already carries Ragweed's earring and Dorsatum's quill. A token of beauty joins those of love and courage—all manifesting aspects of Poppy's developing selfhood. Even as she takes these mementos, Poppy's substance endures. The novel opens with her sneaking out to Bannock Hill to dance with her beloved Ragweed and closes with "Poppy and Rye, [spinning] round and round in a stately waltz, dancing by the light of the moon and the earring, which glittered high on the hazelnut tree" (*Poppy*, 147). Early in her journey, too, Poppy stops to don ladyslippers and indulge in her dream of dancing. At first, dancing symbolizes the fearlessness and freedom that Poppy lacks; ultimately, that freedom becomes a reality she shares with others. Poppy initially wants to dance "in the arms of a handsome mouse" (*Poppy*, 66); yet, at the moment of her greatest discovery—the truth of the stuffed owl and, simultaneously, Mr. Ocax's ruse of protection—Poppy "stood up on her hind legs, leaped into the air, and kicked her heels twice" (*Poppy*, 124) and dances alone. Readers last see Poppy as storyteller to her children as she recites the liberation of Bannock Hill. Recognizing *Poppy* as a choreographed tale of personal and universal dimension, the *Boston Globe-Horn Book* Committee accorded it the 1996 fiction award.

As teller, Avi relates stories of liberation. From the rudimentary versions of *Snail Tale* to the more psychologically gripping

Wolf Rider to the guileless animation of *Poppy*, Avi narrates tales of self-discovery. Story stands as fundamental to Avi's novels. Its nucleus maintains the relative orbit of all other elements of the novel. Although some critics dismiss story as elementary, story is primary and unifying in Avi's work. As E. M. Forster finally acknowledges: "Yes—oh, dear, yes—the novel tells a story" (Forster, 42).

2. Avi as Magician

"Magic"

Today I'm a hill,
tomorrow a sea.
Always wandering
like Miriam's well,
always a bubble
lost in the gorges.

Last night I dreamt
red horses, purple,
green—

In the morning I listened:
an endless babbling of water,
a chatter of parrots.

Today I'm a snail,
tomorrow a giant
palm tree.

Yesterday a cave,
today I'm a seashell.
Tomorrow
I'll be tomorrow.

—Dahlia Rakikovitch, Israel;
translated by Chana Bloch and Ariel Bloch[1]

In fantasy tales and in realistic fiction, Avi sometimes employs
magic to offer his characters new ways of seeing. Magic sets these
works apart from Avi's others, even as it explores his ideological

belief that "... the theme of fiction [is] ... how our vision changes. We see the way we are taught to see. Just because we both have eyes doesn't mean we see the same things. A novel can change what you see."[2] Three of Avi's novels define magic in traditional ways: Magic transforms, a magical setting can explain "otherwise inexplicable events,"[3] and some objects or characters carry magical powers. In *Bright Shadow*, Avi explores both the fantastic and the realistic ways in which magical wishes can alter the course of a human life or the fate of a kingdom. Chris, in *No More Magic*, holds tenaciously to the power of magic to explain the inexplicable, and the three protagonists in *Tom, Babette, and Simon* encounter magical characters that change them. However, for almost-13-year-old Maggie in *Blue Heron*, "[m]agic was *not* to change things. No, magic was a way of keeping things the way they were."[4] On the surface, this idea seems to challenge directly the more typical uses of magic in children's literature. Yet, Maggie, too, learns to see her world and ultimately herself differently.

Bright Shadow

In the opening of *Bright Shadow*, Morwenna appears to be a Cinderella character: ragged and cleaning, in service to someone else. Morwenna seems relatively content with her life, with her apprenticeship to Miss Helga the chambermaid, and with her flirtatious relationship with Swen. An old man, whom readers recognize as the dying Wizard Pindel, ripples her life one day. "Perhaps she went for a dusting cloth. Perhaps it was a bucket ... all she remembers is when she did go into the hallway she found the oldest man she had ever seen."[5] Pindel, knowing that his death approaches and that he must convey the kingdom's last five magical wishes to someone other than the evil King Ruthvin, reaches out to Morwenna. His touch conveys the five wishes.

> Pindel stared at Morwenna with deep, sad eyes. Suddenly, he snatched one of her hands. Where he found the strength, Morwenna didn't know, but it was impossible for her to move. And

his gaze was so intense that Morwenna, no matter how much she wanted to, could not turn away.

In a low, mournful voice, Pindel began to speak. A sweet voice, a soft voice, almost a singing voice, it filled Morwenna with cutting cold.

"The last wishes are here. They will bring thee long life if thou keep thyself from harm, but nothing for thyself. Use them well. Waste them not. Keep them and thyself well hid. Tell no one what thou has or before thy time all, both thee and they, shall be lost. For when the wishes are gone, so too shall thee be." (*Shadow*, 7–8)

Like Maggie, 12-year-old Morwenna wants nothing more than to remain the same; however, Pindel's touch and his transference of the wishes effect changes in her as she begins to grasp his cryptic instructions about the responsibility and protection of the wishes.

Added to Pindel's request for forgiveness at burdening her, Morwenna's desire to rid herself of the wishes—as she finally comprehends their magnitude and the danger they pose to her—demonstrates Morwenna's satisfaction with who she already is. In addition, it illustrates her increasing awareness that each wish she spends moves her closer to her own death. Morwenna unknowingly uses two wishes to resurrect her foolhardy sweetheart, Swen; the third wish she commands to save Gareth's rebellious troops; and the fourth wish she expends in delivering the kingdom.

Morwenna's decision to spend—or to hold—the last wish becomes a decision about her own death or life. No longer diverted by Swen's playfulness and growing arrogance and equally unable to bear the guarded protection of the Robin-Hood-like leader Gareth, Morwenna goes into hiding. As her knowledge about the power of the wishes increases, she develops into a responsible young woman. Morwenna's decisions reveal her acceptance of her new power and the responsibilities accompanying it. Her final decision to hold the wish stems not from her initial desire to stay the same but from her aspiration to grow old, to live a full human life.

Morwenna is shown those two choices early in the novel. Just after Pindel's touch,

Morwenna returned to polishing the king's throne. But as she worked, notions of home slipped away. Her mind drifted back to the old man, and to what she thought he had said, to his gnarled, tapping fingers.

As she puzzled about it all, as she slowly rubbed the smooth, glossy surface of the throne, the wood grew bright enough for her to see her own reflection. Morwenna blinked. Was that *her* face looking back?

The image was of an older woman.

Astonished, Morwenna stared at the face that stared at her. Gradually, it began to change, becoming her face, but as she had been when five years old. Then the image changed again, growing older one moment, younger the next, as if unsure what to be. (*Shadow*, 17)

In choosing to live herself rather than to bestow the wish onto another or put it to any other worthy use, Morwenna becomes sure of what and who to be. That choice stems partly from her magical connection to the natural world.

Blue Heron

As for Maggie, in *Blue Heron*, the natural world carries its own, different, perhaps more powerful, magic. Maggie, too, wants the prerogative to choose—to choose her family, to choose how her time is spent, and, ultimately, to choose between life and death. When Maggie discusses with her father the blue heron she sees in the marshes, he tells her the bird "is thought to be an omen for two things . . . Life. But also, death. You take your pick—according to your desire" (*Heron*, 44). Later, Maggie's questioning "who would pick death?" (*Heron*, 47) reveals her claim to life. Near the novel's end, Maggie "suddenly asked herself, was it the heron who chooses?" (*Heron*, 149). This shift in her thoughts indicates Maggie's exploration of the nature of magic and the magic in nature. Rather than staking the claim to choice that she initially held, like Pindel's touch to Morwenna, Maggie transfers the ability—and the responsibility of choice—to the heron, the magical source.

If Maggie gives up her control as ballast as her family's stability worsens, why does she begin to mimic the heron, to attempt to reach out to it, to touch it? "If she could touch it, all would be well, because touching the magic meant you and the magic became one" (*Heron*, 166). If she could touch the heron, magic would ensure wellness, and the sameness of Maggie's world would persist. However, as Maggie does touch the heron, she realizes the impossibility of her desire for stasis.

> Gradually the distance between them decreased. The heron, as if transfixed, held its place, its eyes staring right at Maggie. Maggie could see now that the bird's colors were much more complex than she had seen from the shore. There were shades of grays, blues, blacks. Even the whites had many shades. She began to see individual feathers, how they were layered, how coarse some were, while others were fine and small. And though the bird was standing still, the tips of some feathers fanned and flowed, ruffling in a breeze that Maggie could not feel." (*Heron*, 166–67)

As the bird remains fixed, Maggie changes. She comes to see the heron's feathers in their complexity; she comes to perceive the complexities of life and of herself. Just as Morwenna chooses life, so Maggie touches the heron's "warmth, its life" (*Heron*, 167).

Ultimately, Maggie's only choice is to go home to her mother and to let her father's broken family heal without her. Still, as her departing act, Maggie seeks out the damaged child, Tucker, who has hunted the heron. She shares with him the secret of touching the heron.

> Very slowly Maggie reached out her hand. Tucker started and drew back. But Maggie continued to move her hand forward slowly. This time Tucker did not move but just stared at her until she touched fingers to his cheek. (*Heron*, 174)

She shares with Tucker the heron's omen of life and—touching him—charges him with it. Readers know from the last page that Tucker takes Maggie's talisman of magic, a prismatic crystal from her mother, to begin to redefine his relationship with the heron—

and perhaps to renegotiate the afflicted relationships in his own family.

Magic also entraps the three central characters in *Tom, Babette, and Simon*. Like Maggie, these three characters begin by believing that if one possesses magic, one need not act, only wish. In the first of the book's "three tales of transformation," Tom, bored with his life, swaps places with Charley the cat, only to learn that the transformation is permanent; a cat's body now houses a 12-year-old boy. Now an unhappy, homeless cat, Tom finds the cat wizard, Peggy, and brings her to Charley to conduct the magic again, to reexchange the places of boy and cat. Tom foolishly trusts the wizard, and Peggy snatches Charley's body. She becomes human, and the two boys remain trapped within cats' bodies, perpetually searching for home.

Maggie, too, searches for home. *Blue Heron* opens with her hoping that nothing has changed with her father, that this home is a reliable one. The summer proves how mutable home and family can be. At the novel's end, Maggie returns home to Seattle, but she carries with her a new awareness of the complications of life, of the complexities of family. She finds that she can like her stepmother and that she could love a baby stepsister. Most important of all, however, Maggie learns that she can no longer cast her father as Merlin the magician, who can fix everything. As Tom begins to realize that he merely wants to be a boy, with all the problems of school and homework, so Maggie discovers that she wants not a magician but simply a father.

Maggie's wishes dictate who her father should be, rather than appreciate who he is. In turn, his vision of their father-daughter relationship, of their summer vacation ambushes Maggie. In part, she fights hard to grow because her father cherishes her changelessness.

Tom, Babette, and Simon

A parent's wishes trap Babette, too. Her mother wants a perfect child, so the witch Esmerelda enables Queen Isabelle to "have a daughter who will appear flawless."[6] Like the Emperor's new clothes, this child is invisible—a fact that drives both mother and father mad. Because these parents want desperately to believe in the reality of their wishes rather than in magic, they ban mirrors, sit in the dark, and bind their eyes. Not believing in the magic— or perhaps because they believe in the truth of the nothingness they see—the king and queen go mad, leaving Babette alone. As she ages, Babette begins to question what she does not see. For her, another act of magic provides an escape from her curse of invisibility. Having only the lies of her people to confirm her visibility, Esmerelda gives Babette magic as a way to the truth. The witch tells Babette that she is invisible; the truth then gives her the mirror of her visibility. Like Lewis Carroll's Alice, Babette walks through the mirror; once on the other side, she constructs an image of herself.

Like Babette's mother, as long as Maggie believes in fantastic magic, in magic as a force wielded by wizards, she is vulnerable to disappointment. Like Babette, Maggie slowly starts to see herself as an agent of change. When she witnesses Tucker's abuse by his father in church and then herself sustains abuse by her father first in a restaurant and then in the car driving home, she must inspect new truths. She moves beyond holding her father to his promise of being Merlin to understanding him as a flawed human being. Perhaps the most important truth Maggie faces is one about herself, a truth she whispers in confession to the heron's secrecy: "The people I love—sometimes—I don't like them" (*Heron,* 164). When nothing happens after she voices these words, Maggie realizes that they are not a curse; they are merely the truth. Maggie becomes like Babette in choosing the powerful, sometimes painful, visibility of truth.

It is the final tale of transformation that offers the most drama.[7] Simon, the hunter, wishes for recognition and the kind of fame that would "have the whole world gaze upon me with admiration and envy" (*Tom,* 74). When he kills the Golden Bird out of greed, he transforms into a bird/man—and gets his wish. Imprisoned in a body half-bird, half-man, Simon becomes the prince's prisoner, an oddity displayed for others' amusement. Yet, even

this recognition wanes as the prince grows tired of Simon and
eventually frees him. Simon returns to his parents, who reject
him because they do not recognize him. When Simon spies the
Golden Bird for a second time, he places himself between the
Golden Bird and the hunter about to kill her. He receives her ultimate grace: She transforms him into a bird, a creature of freedom
who can now "notice the world" (*Tom*, 99). Like Simon, Maggie
gets close enough to the bird to heed its intricate beauty and to
appreciate its freedom. For Simon, the Golden Bird symbolizes
the ominous choice between life and death. In saving the bird, he
chooses death but receives life. Maggie's belief—that if the blue
heron remains safe, then her father will live—urges her to reach
out and touch it. She puts herself between her father and death;
reaching out to touch the heron, therefore, symbolizes reaching
out to her father. Like Simon, Maggie receives the bird's grace,
for in touching it she feels life. Simon and Maggie learn that the
choice is not simply between life and death but concerns noticing
the world and its stunning complexities.

No More Magic

One review of *Tom, Babette, and Simon* states that "Avi has a confident sense of the possibilities of fiction; his stories are rich amal-
gamations of magic, suspense, horror, and philosophy."[8] Nevertheless, the statement fails to mention the humor that permeates
these three stories and *No More Magic* as well. Magic does not
ensnare these characters. Like *Blue Heron*, this is a realistic story
in which a belief in magic fuels the plot. Muffin mourns the loss of
magic in the marriage of her now-absent parents. Her quest to
find it, to give it back to them, propels her to join Chris on his
adventures to recapture the magic he believes others have lost.
Chris's father keeps telling him that there is "no more magic."
But Chris ardently believes in the agents of magic and in typical,
everyday manifestations of it, from Green Lantern rings to war-
locks and witches. Muffin's aunt gets rid of her niece's warlock
suit because she thinks Muffin searches for the black art every-

where. This act further convinces Chris that sorcery is real. After all, why would she give away the suit if it did not have mysterious powers?

Maggie shares this connection to magic through talismen that carry a rather traditional expectation of magical force. She brings to her summer home her copy of *Ancient Tales of Magic* and takes pleasure in her father's decoration of her loft with the stuffed fantasy characters and creatures he has given her over the years, including Merlin the Magician, a unicorn, a dragon, the good witch Glinda, and even a hobbit. Maggie's initial naive belief in fantastic magic closely parallels the cereal-box magic held by Muffin and Chris as they theorize about magic carpets, Druid coats, and pocket magic.

Of course, Chris uses magic only as a tool to help him find his stolen bicycle, which is a spooky shade of green. To solve the mystery, he adopts his father's philosophy of asking the right questions to get the right answers, a successful ploy that works for the characters in *Who Stole the Wizard of Oz?* Maggie, too, uses questioning to solve mysteries. She goes to question her younger neighbor Tucker about his interest in the heron but finds herself pulled into his distraction. In conversations with her stepmother, Joanna, Maggie asks questions. She wants to know "how . . . people get to be the way they are" (*Heron,* 111) and queries Joanna about her father, his relationship with his new family, his medication, and his odd behavior.

Chris solves his mystery, yet the novel's end finds him still believing in a kind of occultism that can explain the inexplicable. Muffin becomes more convinced of the existence of magic when her parents return, reunited. Maggie, however, terms this kind of magic "old magic" (*Heron,* 121) and deems it unable to conquer or even to explain the blunt realities of life. Maggie must find new sources of magic. "Slowly, she picked [her magical creatures and people] up and placed them in a corner of the loft. She would have to think about magic in a different kind of way" (*Heron,* 80). In the blue heron, Maggie discovers the magic of truth, a revelation that allows her to redefine her father as man, not as magician. Like Muffin, Maggie, too, must move beyond a literal definition of

magic and into an expansive understanding of it. Magic is a
potential, a power of belief, not a supernatural force.

"*No More Magic* doesn't have any in the first place but tricks
readers into expecting some. . . . [C]hildren look and hope for
magic in their daily lives, by pretending and/or believing"[9]
Although "this relevant theme is not explored far enough"
(Zarookian, 94) in *No More Magic*, Avi returns to it in *Blue
Heron*. Maggie discovers the magic in her daily life, especially in
the natural world. It offers solace and stillness compared to the
craziness of her father's calls, his frenzy, and her agitated family.
Like Poppy, who sees the intricacies of the forest as she gains
knowledge of herself, Maggie's first visit to the marsh is described
as enchanted. Maggie recounts her original vision of the blue
heron:

> As though coming back to life, the heron slowly lowered its
> neck and began to peer into the water again. The next instant
> the bird plunged its beak into the water and then withdrew it.
> Maggie thought she saw a tiny fish wiggle in the bird's beak. It
> happened so quickly— all in a blur—she could not be sure.
>
> The heron—motionless again—was staring down as before.
>
> Maggie was afraid to move. But she could not stay so still, not
> like the bird. She shifted her feet. The heron's head shot up.
> Once again, it was listening, watching. Involuntarily, Maggie
> cleared her throat.
>
> At the sound the bird spread its enormous wings and, with a
> rush of wind that Maggie felt on her eyes, the bird leaped into
> the air and flew away, its wings flapping slowly, voluptuously.
>
> . . . Maggie walked back to the cottage, entered with caution,
> and climbed into the loft. As she lay in her bed she kept thinking
> of the heron. How beautiful it was. How magical. Never before
> had she experienced such a sense of magic, real magic. (*Heron*,
> 32–33)

Maggie replaces the magnetism of make-believe with nature's
daily wonders.

Still, Maggie accepts that this magic stands as a different sort.
It can offer peace, even privacy and consolation, but it cannot fix
everything. This power carries with it only the possibility of new

ways of seeing. Morwenna perceives Swen's foolishness and notices men's inanities and greed; she also discovers her own tenacity for life as she chooses her life over others' lives. Viewing things newly from a cat's perspective, Tom comprehends the value of the life he gave up. Babette discovers the thrill of visibility and considers herself for the first time as whole, complete, and imperfect. Simon attributes the true value of the Golden Bird to its majestic humility and self-sacrifice, not its monetary value. Although Chris still clings to belief in magic at the novel's end, he recognizes the truth rather than the fiction of Mr. Polder, and his brother Mike no longer has the upper hand in their sibling encounters. At the same time, Maggie sees that her new magic may not present answers; nevertheless, it accents the majesty and the mystery of life. She accepts the ambiguities of human feelings and relationships, learns the vulnerability of growing up, and discovers her own resilience, courage, and reliability. More than any other character's, Maggie's re-visioning of the world culminates in the re-visioning of self. This introspective novel resembles the work of Paula Fox in mood and style. Like Fox, Avi dignifies the complications and complexities of adolescents' lives as he narrates a story about the quiet intensity of changing self. As Hazel Rochman writes in a *Booklist* "Focus" column:

> When you read the lyrical nature descriptions in the quiet parts of this story, it's hard to believe they're by the writer of books like the tight thriller *Wolf Rider*, or the raucous comedy *S.O.R. Losers*, or the jumpy, brilliant school story *Nothing but the Truth*. Then, as this novel continues and scenes of stillness and solitude contrast with raging family confrontation, you realize that Avi is drawing on everything he's written, and more. The telling has the best kind of surprise, reversal that then appears inevitable. There's a rich ambiguity, a yoking of opposites in character, language, mood, pace, and viewpoint that's rare in YA fiction. (Rochman, 930)

Perhaps the uniqueness of this book stems from Avi's regard for young adults. He states: "This is a rare book for me in that I was thinking of someone very specific. I originally used her real name, and it was hard to give that up. She's the daughter of a single parent, a very old friend of my wife's. I do have great affection for the young girl, for the real one and the fictional one. And for the father. I've come to realize that as a writer you have to love your characters. I guess it's the way you love people. You have to take them for what they are" (Rochman, 930). Perhaps this reveals Avi as the greatest magician of all—an author who can "imagine the truth" (Rochman, 930) and transform it into fiction.

3. Avi as Historian

> The advantage of good historical novels over the history that
> emerges from history books . . . can be dramatic. They're mined
> from history yet they are alive. Their characters speak human
> words, think human thoughts, humanly respond to the prob-
> lems and the place in which they live. To this end, the writer
> must embrace history in an act of identification.
>
> —Scott O'Dell[1]

A history major in college, Avi unites interest in and knowledge of
history with his work in children's and young adult literature. He
developed and taught courses in the history of children's literature for undergraduates at Trenton State College and a course in
American children's literature for graduate students at Simmons
College in Boston. Rather than using a textbook, he assembles a
comprehensive range of original literary sources; these pieces
become the text and basis of discussion. Avi articulated a historical view of American children's literature in "Children's Literature: The American Revolution," published in the Winter 1977
edition of *Top of the News*, a professional journal for librarians.
This article challenges the typical understanding of American
children's literature as derived from a British tradition. Avi
argues convincingly that a distinctly American view of childhood—as a unique developmental period with a literature of subversion—forced a break from the British tradition of literature as
a training ground for adulthood.

As a fiction writer, Avi mines the rich veins of history. He combines historical settings with other elements of a novel in many
books. *Something Upstairs* juxtaposes the present with an early

nineteenth-century past in a compelling ghost story. A historical setting serves as backdrop to family drama in *Beyond the Western Sea* (1850) and *The Barn* (1854). *The Man Who Was Poe* (1848) examines a historical figure to explore the creative process, whereas *Punch with Judy* (1874) manipulates the comedic art of the traditional puppet play to reveal tragedy in life. Setting and mimicry unite in *The History of Helpless Harry* (1845) and *Emily Upham's Revenge* (1875), books that effectively parody the melodramatic Victorian vignette. Avi evokes the past to examine and critique social mores in *The True Confessions of Charlotte Doyle* (1832) and *Shadrach's Crossing* (1932). These works, individually and collectively, combine historical moments with personal stories. In these titles, history operates as a pervasive and defining setting; one cannot extract these characters from their historical setting because the societal attitudes of the age dictate each character's behavior, even if that conduct is nonconforming.

Moving beyond the novels' authentic parameters, Avi also realizes the universal, timeless themes of humanity. "Much historical fiction for children works to persuade readers that we are now as humans what we have always been."[2] Examination of the brief period from 1768 to 1783, which serves as background in four of Avi's novels, illuminates this author's ability to historicize and to "dehistoricize" (*Pleasures*, 99) simultaneously.

He writes "[s]omewhere along the line, I can't explain where, I developed an understanding of history not as fact but as story."[3] History becomes story as Avi "[works] hard to make the characters and ideas stay with the readers long after the last page."[4] *Night Journeys* (1768), *Encounter at Easton* (1768), *The Fighting Ground* (1778), and *Captain Grey* (1783) offer readers the "act of identification" with characters in conflict with their societies.

In each of these four books, the American society in revolution against the British establishes a historical setting that places the young people in a society characterized by an ideology of dissension. How does this fact influence the individual characters? At what points do the characters adopt and act out the spirit of revolution?

Night Journeys

Night Journeys' "strength ... is [Avi's] insightful portrayal of appealing, uncommon characters and the generally believable growth which they experience. . . ."⁵ The opening line of *Night Journeys* immediately defines the tenor of conflict that permeates the novel's characters and attitude: "My name is Peter York. I place here before you the testimony of the great crisis in my life, how it came to pass and what was the result."⁶ The indentured British servants Elizabeth Mawes and Robert Linnly launch the plot and charge Peter's spirit of defiance when they revolt against their American master by running away to seek freedom. Only through bondage could they escape imprisonment in Great Britain; however, once in America, the 12-year-old girl and 10-year-old boy embrace a culture of independence and resistance that fuels their flight.

Unlike Elizabeth and Robert, who act out of moral imperative and precedent, Peter is motivated by a false sense of enslavement and a skewed definition of freedom. The orphaned Peter resents his adoptive father, the Quaker farmer Everett Shinn. He states: "I did not know why he had taken me in, other than because I would be required to work for him. I came to him with nothing but my ability to labor and the single inheritance of my horse" (*Night*, 6). Peter perceives himself as victim; therefore, he considers Mr. Shinn his antagonist and an obstacle to his freedom. In contrast to the servitude of Elizabeth and Robert, Peter enjoys great independence. Although he has duties to perform on the farm, he moves about unhindered. The Shinns place upon him only their reasonable expectations of a 12-year-old boy who is a responsible member of their family.

As Peter interprets Mr. Shinn's silence and reserve as an unspoken judgment about him, Mr. Shinn becomes the object of Peter's revolt. Peter's rebellion takes the form of conformity: In joining the search party for the runaway bondsboy and bondsgirl, Peter rejects Mr. Shinn's nonviolent beliefs and opts to participate in a lawful, yet potentially violent, activity. In so doing, Peter's personal rebellion targets Mr. Shinn even as it affirms slavery by seeking to capture and punish those who, like Peter, have rebelled.

Mr. Shinn and Peter enlist in the search for the escaped servants for different motivations. The "thought of the reward caught [Peter's] mind and inflamed it. Twelve pounds! *There* was the needed horse!" (*Night*, 11) Peter grasps greedily for the American dream: With money comes ownership; with ownership comes freedom. Not knowing that the escapees are in fact children slightly younger than he is, the thrill of a chase excites Peter, who takes his gun in preparation for the hunt. Peter joins in a game, whereas Mr. Shinn "as Justice of the Peace . . . was obliged to know and render all assistance" (*Night*, 10). Moreover, Peter thinks in moral extremes: The captives broke the law first in England, then in America. Peter lacks the ability to distinguish between classes of crimes and their seriousness; in Peter's eyes, guilt is guilt. The opposite holds true for Mr. Shinn. In part, his Quaker beliefs dictate nonviolent, peaceful actions. On the other hand, Mr. Shinn understands moral ambiguity; he knows the runaways are children who committed a petty crime that resulted in their indentured status—facts that suggest they be treated differently. The author combines documented facts about the Quaker stance against slavery with the specifics of Mr. Shinn's character. Mr. Shinn recognizes that enforcing the law that binds him simultaneously places him in conflict with himself and with the higher moral law to which he subscribes.

Avi allows each of these characters to develop in their complexities. Peter comes to understand moral ambiguity even as Mr. Shinn realizes that his own conflict cannot be resolved. Mr. Shinn participates half-heartedly in the search, yet allows the captured Robert to escape. In such contradictory actions, he satisfies both lawful and moral belief systems. Paralyzed by the tension between lawful and moral imperatives, Mr. Shinn transfers the responsibility for action to Peter. The concluding pages of the novel show Mr. Shinn enabling Peter to ensure the escape of Robert and Elizabeth. Mr. Shinn can act as only an accomplice to Peter's crime even as he wishes Peter to break "the law [that]

says thee are equally guilty if thee help a bondsman escape"
(*Night*, 134). Despite the indirectness of Mr. Shinn's speech,
Peter comes to recognize the man's intention. "[S]tanding in the
middle of the road, standing absolutely still" (*Night*, 135) proves
to be an action whose meaning Peter comprehends. Peter's conviction in aiding Elizabeth and Robert to escape on his horse
gains affirmation in Shinn's stance. That affirmation provokes
Peter's realization that, although "[t]hey had their freedom . . . in
that same moment, I knew I did not want mine" (*Night*, 135).

This final scene epitomizes Peter's new understanding of Mr.
Shinn's morality even as it evinces pivotal changes in Peter himself. Initially motivated by reward and excited by the hunt, Peter
eventually recognizes his own complicity in evil. When Peter discovers Elizabeth, he thinks:

> The longer I sat there, the more that sense of triumph grew,
> unfurling gaudy images within my mind of my return home. I
> saw myself bringing the girl to Mr. Shinn's house, claiming the
> reward for her capture, a great victory that would wipe away my
> other failings. The more I thought of it, the more it pleased me
> and the more I knew what I wanted to do. So it was that I
> decided to pretend to have noticed nothing [not the brand of
> felony on her hand] and find a way to get her to return home
> with me. (*Night*, 171–72)

Images of successful revolutions and heroic returns continue to
mark Peter's definitions of victory. These visions of glory
notwithstanding, Peter impulsively shoots Elizabeth when he
thinks she has run away from him. His initial reaction is one of
paralyzing horror. Unable to move, he merely stands there. Eventually, Peter approaches Elizabeth and confronts not only the
results of his action but also knowledge of himself.

> When I picked her up, she moaned. What her cry when I shot
> her had not done, what her blood had not done, that one sound
> accomplished. I began to cry, great sobbing cries that shook me.
> I was crying for her, and for myself, tears I had not allowed
> myself when I was most alone. (*Night*, 78)

Peter's dreams of glory are grounded; he no longer seeks the reward, no longer thrills in the hunt. Rather, he asks for forgiveness and determines to aid Elizabeth and Robert.

Consumed by the burden of his guilt, Peter still misinterprets Mr. Shinn's actions. Mr. Shinn tells Peter to join in the search party for the girl partly because he trusts Peter to lead them in the wrong direction; however, Peter takes this instruction as impetus to leave, to join the runaways, to "flee with them to Easton" (*Night*, 101).

To this point, certainty has defined Peter's decisions. He acts, he does not question. He judges Mr. Shinn despite not understanding him. He recognizes his own ability to commit evil, but he does not see his own potential—or that of others—for good. When Mr. Shinn facilitates Peter's escape by bringing the horse, Peter begins to question. He queries Mr. Shinn about the extent to which he will uphold the law and about what he expects of Peter. For the first time, Peter admits to not knowing definitively Mr. Shinn's expectations and motivations. He becomes unsure about Mr. Shinn. That doubt evidences Peter's transformation from "simplistic moralism"[7] to discernment of moral ambiguity. He abandons his escape and decides to return home instead, a decision about which he feels ambiguous.

> "I must go back."
> "Are you sure?"
> "No," I admitted. "But I must." (*Night*, 139)

The book ends where it began, with Peter's recognition of the significance of this period of his life.

Encounter at Easton

The testimonial format that opened *Night Journeys* persists in the novel's sequel, *Encounter at Easton*. The court recorder, the British lord to whom he reports, and the date of and reason for his reporting remain undisclosed. The conceit serves no purpose other than to shape the novel's format. *Encounter at Easton* opens with "the recorded Testimony of three men and a boy, taken down as they spoke at some sort of hearing in the spring of 1768."[8] Rather than presenting the four accounts individually, Avi organizes them "in order that it might read as a tale" (*Encounter*, 4). The alternating points of view convey an "energetic, understated, slightly formal style that heightens the tension and underscores the tragic climax. . . ."[9]

Peter York makes no appearance here, although the runaway Robert Linnly confesses to using Peter's name to protect his identity. Despite being the continued story of his escape to freedom, Robert's narrative does not appear until the third chapter. John Tolivar, the labor contractor who "purchased" (*Encounter*, 9) Elizabeth and Robert, makes a single statement. Although this statement reveals Tolivar's character—and validates readers' dislike of him as they knew him in *Night Journeys*—it functions primarily to advance plot. Through Tolivar, the character of Nathaniel Hill, a "gentleman" bounty hunter, enters the novel and instigates the story's telling.

Both Nathaniel Hill and Robert Linnly start their testimony by referring to Elizabeth. Hill begins by stating his innocence in "wishing to do the girl harm" (*Encounter*, 5), while Robert sincerely claims, "I will tell you what happened to Elizabeth" (*Encounter*, 14). Because readers of *Night Journeys* know that Elizabeth bears a gunshot wound from Peter York, these openings increase suspense at what happens to the girl and how others perceive the course of events. It dramatizes less Robert's journey to freedom than it stages Elizabeth's death. When Nathaniel Hill, trailing Elizabeth, hires Robert to run his chores, the narrative strand of Robert's escape entwines with Hill's search.

Readers learn about the pre-Revolutionary society of Easton, Pennsylvania, from the ways in which characters narrate their parts. The three chapters from Constable Clagget demonstrate how law supported a system of indentured slavery. Clagget follows procedures that reward men like Nathaniel Hill for lawfully pursuing bondsmen. Clagget's matter-of-fact testimony contrasts with Hill's self-conscious, self-righteous statement. A product of his times, Hill assumes the airs of a gentleman, despite behaving like a scoundrel. He dismisses the town as "not particularly civilized. . . . Considerable activity was centered on a muddy market street with homes and shops in a thick and filthy cluster" (*Encounter*, 30). Across the river from Trenton, New Jersey, Easton promises freedom and the safety of anonymity to Robert and Elizabeth. Seemingly, it offered the same to a woman known as "Mad Moll." Raped by a French soldier during the French-American war, Moll runs away to Trenton.

> "No one would have me then. No one. I could not stay. How could I? No one wanted me. My parents, the man I was to marry. I came here. I've been here for some time. I don't see people. They don't wish to see me." (*Encounter*, 53)

Moll experiences the same ostracism in Easton, a community that also labels her lunatic and considers her a curiosity living on the town's outskirts.

In turn, Moll harbors the runaways Elizabeth and Robert. She plays a kindly witch to their Hansel and Gretel. Moll discovers the delirious Elizabeth resting on a bank while Robert has gone into town. Conveying Elizabeth to her cave-home, she treats her wounds with herbs and homemade remedies and calls Elizabeth her daughter. She welcomes Robert because he declares himself as Elizabeth's friend and demonstrates remarkable affection and concern for the young girl. The three form a vulnerable, misunderstood community of outcasts.

Nevertheless, that community of three is short-lived. Nathaniel Hill lawfully enlists the aid of Constable Clagget to apprehend Elizabeth with the intention of returning her to Tolivar for the 20-pound reward, which will enable him to pay off his debt. In the dramatic final scene, Robert holds Hill's stolen gun on Hill and Clagget while Moll bears the dying Elizabeth out of the cave. Moll trips, Elizabeth free-falls down the hill, and Hill shoots, killing Moll. Recognizing the symbiosis between Moll and Elizabeth, Robert insists upon their burial together. The innkeeper Grey buys Robert Linnly's contract from Tolivar. Robert "thus remains in Easton with a new master" (*Encounter*, 137). Although Avi presents Grey as a decent man, readers cannot help but wonder if this new home and this new master will simply become a new form of servitude.

Captain Grey

That question takes on additional potency in light of *Captain Grey*, its characters, and its concerns with forms of slavery. The novel's format unites history with character; however, one reviewer contends that "[t]hough in the past, the characters would not be all that out of place today. . . ."[10] Genuine affection between two children characterizes the caring relationship between Robert and Elizabeth, and, like so many children today, they depend upon each other because the adult world consistently proves itself unsafe and unreliable. Rapacious characters like Nathaniel Hill stand ready to take advantage of others' misfortunes. And good people like the tapman Grey also occasionally step in to assume the responsibilities and kindnesses others have neglected. Unlike *Night Journeys*, this novel draws clear lines between good and evil; the characters align themselves with immediate recognizability. As a result, the novel describes a static encounter between the "good guys" and the "bad guys" rather than a journey of growth.

The times and places that permitted indentured servitude mold the boy Robert Linnly into the man Captain Grey. Robert regresses from a sympathetic, decent character in *Night Journeys* and *Encounter at Easton* into a sort of Mad Moll in *Captain Grey*. In the original edition of *Captain Grey*, Avi describes the Captain as "Connecticut born . . . an American."[11] In the edition reissued 16 years later, Avi rewrites that passage and clearly attributes Robert Linnly's lineage to Captain Grey:

> "I was English born," he said softly, "but like a slave was shipped when a boy to America for what others call a crime, the stealing of a trinket. Set free, I became an American, as good as any other. . . ." (*Grey*, 129)

This stands as the only change Avi makes in the text of this novel. Although Avi did not overtly conceive of *Captain Grey* as a continuation of Robert Linnly's story, naming Linnly's caretaker Grey establishes a connection between the two characters and the two novels that Avi capitalizes upon later.

Seeing Captain Grey as Robert Linnly—and Robert Linnly as Captain Grey—charges readers to view a character on a historical continuum that is both personal and societal. Knowledge of Robert Linnly's early life provides readers with a measure of understanding for the madness of Captain Grey. Linnly's experiences as an indentured servant, his attempt to escape, and the loss of Elizabeth—even his return to labor with the innkeeper Grey—establish Captain Grey's loathing of slavery. As a whole, then, these three novels constitute Avi's first observations that slavery promoted only inhumanity.

In some ways, *Captain Grey* employs the folktale motif of Hansel and Gretel again. Kevin Cartwright assumes the role of Hansel, captured by the witchlike Captain Grey and imprisoned in an attic room; his sister Cathleen plays Gretel, the resourceful girl who enjoys relative freedom as she struggles to survive and who produces the downfall of the villain. Avi elaborates on this pattern by giving it a historical reality.

The year 1783 finds 11-year-old Kevin and 13-year-old Cathleen newly reacquainted with their father. "When the war [of independence] was over, our father, whom we had not heard from or seen for seven years, came back to claim us" (*Grey*, 4). On their move to the remote wilderness of New Jersey, a band of pirates attacks the family, killing the father and kidnapping Kevin. Kevin presumes his sister Cathleen dead (as she does him) and narrates this story from his attic prison.

Kevin relates the pirate adventure with enough detail to make it historically believable. While Kevin's language will be familiar to contemporary readers, occasional words and phrases achieve a particular historical cadence. He reports that, during his sailing instruction, he "rather fancied that the bird took interest" (*Grey*, 24) and that he and Jacob "were being tossed in every direction, but he would not quit my lesson" (*Grey*, 55); in addition, he defines the cannon's trunnion as soon as he uses the word (*Grey*, 123). However, it is the technology of Captain Grey's piracy that places the historical setting. Their boats run under manpower, not motors; they keep lookout over the bay from the highest point on land, not from the air; their weaponry consists of shot and powder stored away from living quarters and raft-bound cannons.

"Anyone looking for a hearty old-fashioned swashbuckler should certainly sign on with *Captain Grey*" because Avi adds "a neat twist"[12] to the traditional pirate adventure story. These are land-bound pirates living in Captain Grey's Free Nation. Just as their motivation remains obscure, so their plunder seems meaningless except as decoration for their huts. The captain maintains his crew intentionally outside the boundaries of society; therefore, their booty cannot be exchanged or sold for monetary gain. These pirates take no prisoners because they do not risk leaving witnesses.

The book draws on history to create character and setting. It also develops characters whose individuality allows Avi to explore universal human themes. The book's irony centers on Captain Grey himself. In one of his many traitorous commands during the war, the Captain unwittingly destroys his family. He flees from this action and turns traitor again but does not accept personal responsibility for his crime. He incorporates anger and redirects it inappropriately into other avenues of war. The captain peoples his Free Nation with British prisoners of war. As he explains to Kevin,

> They were British citizens to the man, and not one, *not one* had come to fight willingly. Each of them had been taken against his will to fight a war he did not want. Weren't these men also slaves?
>
> I set them free. And brought them here. . . . All the men I've ever seen are slaves to other men, to governments or such. The only man who's truly free is the one who is part of nothing, and wars against the rest of the world. (*Grey*, 131)

Freeing these men from a slavery he perceives, ironically he proceeds to enslave them to his authority. The Captain seizes Kevin as prisoner, too, yet his reasons for doing so can be nothing but depraved. Despite his declaration to educate Kevin, to treat him like a son, and to train him for taking over the Free Nation, the Captain's greater commitment to "nothing" excludes all possibilities of genuine relationships.

Until Kevin reconnects with Cathleen, the novel's consistent voice of sanity, he becomes complicitous in the captain's derangement. Kevin participates in his second battle, an attack on a schooner, with full knowledge of the assault's intention and consequences.

> I suppose I could have sat down and refused to go. It remains on my conscience that I did not. The truth is, however, that the longer I was with the captain and his gang, the more I felt a part of it, so that despite my inner hatred I went along unwillingly. (*Grey*, 83)

Even though Kevin thinks that he could have done nothing else, that he "was very young and very much at the mercy of the captain" (*Grey*, 83), readers see that Kevin has other options. He chooses not to refuse; then, like the captain, he excuses himself and charges someone else with the responsibility for his actions. Both the captain and Kevin place the burden of their guilt on the institution of slavery; they never acknowledge that abnegation of personal responsibility only fortifies slavery. In a sense, they become their own captors as they perpetuate the very system against which they rail.

Kevin invites readers to excuse him also because of his age. However, Avi offers no such pardon as he reveals Kevin in other capacities as resourceful and questioning. From his attic room, Kevin trains a pigeon to carry his messages; in the free time the captain gives him, he searches for ways to free himself and, eventually, to find his sister Cathleen. As counterpoint to Kevin, Cathleen marries responsibility to resourcefulness. Her vision extends beyond her freedom and Kevin's to insist upon the destruction of the captain's sinister nation. She risks her own emancipation to implement the undoing of this evil.

The novel's final scene is disturbing. Kevin knowingly misidentifies Captain Grey from the Free Nation's casualties, allowing the captain possible escape. The decision haunts Kevin, but why? He acknowledges the captain's wrongdoing even as he confesses that, "in spite of myself, recollecting that I was never positive of his fate, while I cannot wish him well, I wish him a life to live" (*Grey*, 141). Yet, because Kevin acknowledges that life as one of "greatest pain" (*Grey*, 141), does he wish the captain forgiveness or damnation? Does he set the captain free or imprison him in self-created torture? Readers must come to their own decisions about the conclusion of Kevin's moral struggle.

The Fighting Ground

The Fighting Ground incorporates pieces from each of these three works of historical fiction in an unbroken mosaic of a society and an individual. Here, Avi instills Jonathan with Peter York's revolutionary spirit and difficult relationship with a father figure; he modifies the reportorial format of *Encounter at Easton* with the time-sequence narration of *Captain Grey*; he further explores Captain Grey's discernment that war makes soldiers into slaves. This backdrop of the American Revolution defines time, event, plot, and characters. "Avi has again written a tale that, through the moral dilemmas faced by an ordinary, believable youngster, makes the past vividly real."[13]

Like Peter York, Jonathan does not understand his father. Jonathan listens eagerly for the ringing of the town's bells to call the civilian militia to battle to take back Trenton (New Jersey) from the Hessians. Despite awareness that his father's participation in an earlier battle wounded him for life, Jonathan misinterprets the apprehension in his father's eyes not as fear for Jonathan's well-being but as cowardice: "His father was afraid, but he wasn't."[14] This judgment enables him to ignore his father's warning, to answer the toll, and to join in the campaign against Trenton.

The novel adopts a journalistic format to chronicle Jonathan's slow awakening to the horrors of war, the very loss of innocence his father feared as inevitable. Jonathan's departure from and return to home take no more than two days. Rather than breaking the story into short chapters (as in the other novels discussed in this chapter), Avi clocks the movement from April 3 to April 4, 1778, with intervals that range from a minute to hours. Like Peter York, Jonathan initially subscribes to war as a glorious, exciting occupation. He views the mounted corporal as a valiant leader into victory. Surprised that the other men in his band are nervous and frightened at the prospect of battle, Jonathan overlooks the corporal's manipulativeness. The corporal reminds readers of Captain Grey in his imperative to fight; he never releases the men, and they become his slaves: his sacrifice—in war and to war. Slowly, Jonathan heeds the discrepancies in the corporal's promises and, all too late, realizes they have been led into a mismatched skirmish. Frightened, untrusting, and unable to defend himself, Jonathan runs. Alone and exhausted, "he was alive and wished that he was dead, but not being dead, he was scared that he might die" (*Fighting*, 55).

That aloneness ends with his capture by three Hessian soldiers. The time spent with the Hessians alters Jonathan's view of war even more. He does not understand their language. Avi's inclusion of the untranslated German within the narrative heightens the tension as it forces most readers to share Jonathan's terror at incomprehension. Similarly, it accents the confusion these soldiers must feel in a strange land. The translation of the German in a postscript further humanizes the soldiers as it voices their fears and conveys their sense of humor, their confusion, their decency. The additional context allows readers to recognize Jonathan's misinterpretations of the Hessians' conversations as singular and panic driven.

Jonathan's captivity shifts from one of stark terror to one of comradeship with these men. All are engaged in a war they no longer want to fight. They take refuge in a farmhouse and establish a comfortable, if short-lived, domestic safety. "Jonathan tried to rekindle his hatred, but all he could muster was the desire to stand close to them, to be taken care of" (*Fighting*, 64). This unlikely community deepens when Jonathan discovers the bodies of the poor farmer and his wife. Jonathan's conviction that the Hessians killed them is shaken somewhat when the soldiers assist him in digging their grave.

Jonathan divorces himself from being a "true soldier" (*Fighting*, 103) when he decides to escape while the Hessians sleep. Jonathan entertains the option of killing the soldiers. " 'Do it,' he heard himself say yet again. 'It's your duty' " (*Fighting*, 103). Unlike Kevin Cartwright, who excuses himself for knowing participation in Captain Grey's evil, Jonathan chooses not to kill the soldiers—himself. However, he acts not out of moral compassion for these men but out of his own fear of killing, a horror that shames him. Jonathan continues to believe that enemies in war deserve death, and he determines to bring the corporal to kill the soldiers.

Not a true soldier, but still committed to war, Jonathan confesses to the corporal his weakness. On the return to the farmhouse, Jonathan "struggle[s] against the monstrous idea that had formed in his mind" (*Fighting*, 121) as the indiscriminate inhumanity of war strikes him. Jonathan now knows that the corporal killed the innocent farmer and his wife and eagerly pursues the three Hessian soldiers, the men to whom Jonathan now feels some connection. Not only can Jonathan not run away from this mission but he also cannot deny this new comprehension of human cruelty. Despite Jonathan's efforts to save them, the Hessians are killed. In a symbolic renunciation of war, Jonathan throws away his borrowed gun. He returns home alive but unspared and innocence lost to the knowing eyes of his father.

Avi employs the American Revolution to examine the horrors of war itself and the transformation it effects in an individual. In doing his research, Avi uncovered a shocking detail about Dr. Warren, the leader of the Americans troop during the battle of Bunker Hill: Dr. Warren's body "had been so dismembered and disemboweled, the only way he could be identified was by the nature of his teeth. And it was Paul Revere who did it" (Benson, 11). This startling, lesser known particular dramatizes for Avi the ghastliness inherent in war. More so than in any other book, *The Fighting Ground* historicizes and dehistoricizes simultaneously. It "makes the war personal and immediate; not [just] history or event, but experience; near and within oneself, and horrible."[15] It is not surprising, then, that Avi dedicates this book to his sons with love, for the novel communicates the exact message that Jonathan's father was to transmit to his son.

Most reviews of this novel place it within the literary tradition of other classic Revolutionary War novels, such as *My Brother Sam is Dead*, *April Morning*, and *Johnny Tremain*. *The Fighting Ground* receives only positive comparison to these other books. However, it is Avi the historian, not Avi the novelist, who articulates the fluidity of history: "If you read a book like *Johnny Tremain*, written in a different period, the forties, you see the tendency to glorify the ideals and values of the American Revolution. I don't think we would look at it in the same simple, unconflicted way today."[16] Indeed, *The Fighting Ground* provokes a decidedly intricate, multivalent examination of war itself, not only of war in history.

Avi met Scott O'Dell shortly after *The Fighting Ground* was selected for the 1985 Scott O'Dell Award for Historical Fiction. "In discussing Avi, O'Dell expressed his hope that this young writer would continue the work he had begun and 'keep historical fiction alive' for young people. Promising talent was all around, he explained, 'but perhaps none like Avi.' If he continues working in the genre, O'Dell predicted, he will 'assume the legacy' of historical fiction master."[17] Not only has he assumed the legacy, but he has also advanced the form.

4. Avi as Stylist

The poet's eye, in a fine frenzy rolling,
Doth glance from heaven to earth, from earth to heaven;
and as imagination bodies forth
The forms of things unknown, the poet's pen
Turns them to shapes, and gives to aery nothing
A local habitation and a name.
That if it would but apprehend some joy,
It comprehends some bringer of that joy;
Or in the night, imagining some fear,
How easy is a bush suppos'd a bear!

—William Shakespeare, "A Midsummer Night's Dream"[1]

Avi participated in "Masquerade," a graduate student summer symposium in literature for children and young adults at Simmons College in 1991. His talk explored the metaphor of mask as essential to the writer's ability to envision the lives and articulate the stories of his characters. In an essay titled "Seeing Through the I,"[2] Avi develops these revelations. In it he offers reflective insights on his conscious stylistic intentions and variations. In a biographical sketch, Avi states that "the historical novel is a curious construction. It represents history but it's not truly accurate. It's a style."[3] Avi adds the masks of comedy and tragedy to the guise of historical fiction. In *Emily Upham's Revenge*, *The History of Helpless Harry*, *Something Upstairs*, and *The Man Who Was Poe*, Avi the historian meets Avi the stylist.

Emily Upham's Revenge; Or, How Deadwood Dick Saved the Banker's Niece: A Massachusetts Adventure and *The History of Helpless Harry: To Which Is Added a Variety of Amusing and Entertaining Adventures* exploit Avi's extensive knowledge of the history of children's literature. Reviews of these two books refer to significant historical developments in children's literature. Analyses of *Emily Upham's Revenge* describe it as "as syrupy and moralistic as were the children's books of the era in which this is set [1875],"[4] as a "spoof of books of the Alger vintage,"[5] and as "an engaging spoof on the old dime novels."[6] Similarly, recognizing its connections to the development of children's literature, reviewers of *The History of Helpless Harry* describe the book as a "literary conceit, mocking the conventions and sentiments of old-time fiction,"[7] as using "the orotund language of the period (1845),"[8] and as comparable to the work of the contemporary historical novelist Leon Garfield.[9] These critiques place the books within not just one but a number of historical traditions. Avi does not merely take a specific work of children's fiction and rework it; rather, the scope of his knowledge of the evolution of children's literature enables him to draw on trends and types. Therefore, rather than retelling a Horatio Alger rags-to-riches story, for example, Avi imbues the character of Seth Marple, Emily Upham's "savior," with some Algerian attributes. This frees the author from the obligation to mirror a story in its retelling and allows him simultaneously to incorporate numerous elements from historical children's literature. Avi stated that one of the ways in which he taught himself to write was through imitation.[10] In these two works, Avi imitates, but he does not replicate. His versions heighten the hyperbole inherent in the original forms.

Emily Upham's Revenge

Emily Upham's Revenge incorporates a variety of historical elements. Seth Marple reads dime novels, and the book itself adopts an "inventively convoluted plot . . . rich with ironies and surprises" (*Dictionary*, 191). When her family falls upon difficult financial times, Emily, seven years old, is sent from her Boston home to stay with her wealthy uncle in North Brookfield, Massachusetts. Because Seth Marple has been sinking the mail rather than delivering it for the meager wages paid by the postmaster,

Mr. Marryat, Emily's uncle never meets her. Instead, the new runaway Seth meets her.

> Seth, who had dark hair and eyes, was not very tall for his eleven years. He wore no shoes and no shirt, just overalls. He also was not what Emily called clean. In fact, Emily Upham had never seen anyone quite like him before, or certainly not so close.[11]

Seth introduces himself as Deadwood Dick, his favorite dime novel hero, and sets out to rescue Emily from her uncle, the man who has sentenced Seth to the workhouse for not delivering the mail, who "as far as Seth was concerned . . . was a thief, a real bandit" (*Emily*, 41). Seth imagines a book in which his masquerade as Deadwood Dick, who saves the banker's niece, yields him delicious revenge. Seth even adopts the persona of Deadwood Dick: He brings Emily to his secret hideout, where he provides her shelter, food, and even a Bible and stool, "gifts [he hoped] would bring pleasure to Emily" (*Emily*, 52). Seth remains true to his mother, fretting at the pain he causes her. Despite the haphazard living arrangement of his bandit hideout in the woods, Seth earns Emily's friendship, respect, and prayers: "[B]less this boy, who is the truest, most fearless and honest boy I have ever met, even though he is so awfully dirty" (*Emily*, 38–41).

Seth intends to rob Upham's bank and to give the money to Emily to send her back to Boston. Emily has promised Seth that her father will be so pleased at her return that he will reward Seth greatly. This plan spurs a story plot full of an "amusing assortment of misadventures and entanglements . . . involving blackmail, fraud, and treachery" (*Dictionary*, 191). As Emily joins in his plans, Seth begins to see beneath her uppity moralistic attitude and her prissiness.

> Aside from the clean dress, she was, by his lights, looking more human every day. Her hair was unkempt, her hands and face weren't the awful white they were when he first met her, her stockings hung limp, and her shoes were scuffed. (*Emily*, 86)

Both Emily and Seth demonstrate commitment to truthtelling. Schooled in the necessity of telling the truth, Emily acts out of rigorous polarities; she parrots the adults' didactic lessons on veracity. Reciting the supremacy of the truth as an ideal, Emily asserts her belief in the poem "Don't tell a lie," whereas Seth arrives at truth through experience.

> "Well," said Seth, "I'll be straight with you. I've tried 'em both, rods and lies. It's not like your poem says at all. I mean, it's a pretty poem and such, and you spoke it good, but the rod hurts a whole lot more. A whole lot." (*Emily*, 90)

He knows the manipulative nature of truth. He does not lie to Emily, but he tells only partial truths to achieve the results he wants. Readers recognize Seth's cleverness in this use of language, as they perceive what his language conceals—and what it reveals. He describes banker Upham as a thief, initially because he holds others' money, yet the story proves the truth of Seth's assessment when the banker orchestrates a robbery of his own bank. Seth and Emily, then, interpret truth and lies differently. However, by the novel's end, the more cultured Emily learns how to hide the truth without lying. She reports that she knows where the stolen money is: " 'It's gone,' she said simply" (*Emily*, 63). When asked a direct question about the money, she replies: " 'I cannot tell a lie, . . . [b]ut I will not tell the truth, either' " (*Emily*, 164). Emily allows everyone to believe that she has burned the money, even though she never directly makes that statement as fact. Emily discovers that to "keep [her] spirit pure and whole" (as the last line of the poem advises), she must keep some of the truth to herself. In fact, Emily returns home with the stolen four thousand dollars "and hid it in a safe place. Each week at church she placed a sealed white envelope containing some of the bills into the charity box. In time all the money was gone" (*Emily*, 172). Emily's hidden truth, then, permits her to uphold the greater personal truth, her belief that money is the root of all evil, a reality her experience proves accurate.

Avi's reading of Mark Twain's *The Adventures of Tom Sawyer* clues readers into an essential historical connection to *Emily Upham's Revenge*, a book Avi dedicates to his twin sister Emily. Avi writes

Tom Sawyer is not just a bad boy in the Aldrich [author of *The Story of a Bad Boy*] sense of the word, a young human with frailties who will nonetheless grow up to be a solid citizen. Importantly, Tom Sawyer lives a boyhood which is manifestly *superior* to adulthood. In this sense the book is ultimately critical of adult society. The adult world, says Tom, is virtually all hypocrisy. Childhood is freedom. Freedom is getting away from the adult world. Childhood is life. Adulthood is a kind of death.[12]

Seth Marple's truthtelling reveals his critical understanding of the adult world's hypocrisy. To escape the civilizing influences of his mother, of Mr. Farnlee, and of other authorities in his society, Seth establishes his secret hideout, a place he shares only with another child, Emily. In this place he lives a life that is superior to the strictures and controls of adult life. He lives off the land and eats only when he wants to eat. Emily enters, bringing with her the blemishes of adult life. She wants to organize, to furnish, to clean, to educate with the Bible. She brings a trunk full of proper clothing, the costumes of the adult world. Nevertheless, Seth's hideout of childhood freedom exerts its influence on Emily. She gets dirty, she begins to participate in the robbery plans, and, ultimately, she steals the black-boxed money. When Emily confronts her father with her knowledge of his thieving, thus exposing his lie, she recognizes the hypocrisy of the adult world. Emily Upham's final act asserts revenge against that pretense of virtue.

Although Emily cannot retrieve the freedom of childhood, Seth Marple tries. Of course, his imagination has enabled him to enjoy a less hampered childhood to begin with. In creating the hideout, Seth realizes a place for childhood's safety. The novel's end finds Seth living with his mother and her new husband, the preacher Mr. Farnlee. Still, Seth reaches out to the freedom of childhood. Although they "moved to the house next door to the church . . . Seth hid his dime novels in the attic, where he continued to read them" (*Emily*, 171). Deadwood Dick will live on in Seth's unrestrained imagination.

Just as Seth Marple refers to Tom Sawyer, so does Horatio Stockton Edgeworth yearn for the freedom from adult restraints that Seth enjoys.

Eleven years of age, Harry had a smooth round face, a face that always seemed to be poking out from beneath a cap he never would take off. His hands were mostly in trouser pockets. His feet seemed to slip rather than step. And yes, he did have dark, soft eyes and an appealing mouth, all of which made many people consider him small, hopeless, and helpless—a boy in constant need of protection.[13]

Although this description purports to be in the third person and written from the same omniscient point of view as is *Emily Upham's Revenge*, the novel's structure and opening distinguish it. A table of contents outlines *Emily Upham's Revenge,* and eight of the ten chapter titles emphasize the hyperbolic nature of the spoof with exclamation points.

The History of Helpless Harry

Keeping the extensive subtitle borne by *Emily Upham's Revenge,* Avi mimics the Victorian novel differently in *The History of Helpless Harry*. In many ways, Avi's imitation becomes criticism, an element that anticipates his exploration of metafiction in later works.

The History of Helpless Harry numbers each chapter, then titles it with a plot description. An example is chapter 1, "in which we begin by introducing a hero named Harry; a look, too, at his dignified parents; also, a most important question is asked" (*Harry,* 3). By using the word "we," this introduction immediately draws the reader into collusion with the writer/narrator as separate from his characters. Furthermore, it designates Harry as the hero, despite the narrator's decidedly unheroic description of hopeless, helpless Harry, and points to the presence of Harry's parents as characters in the tale. Finally, the subheading tantalizes the reader with its vague plot-teaser. Therefore, although the subtitle imitates older fiction in its summary, it also withholds important information. In addition, some elements of the subtitle can be understood in their full ironic potential only when the novel has been completed. Here, readers of the book learn a

"Seth Marple" lesson late in the novel when they realize that Harry's parents only appear to be dignified.

The narrator places himself at the center of the book with the opening line "I will begin my story . . ." (*Harry*, 3). Because the narrator consistently speaks directly to the reader, this insistence on presence emerges as a significant pattern throughout the novel. The technique directs one's reading of the story through chapter subtitles; it separates the narrator and the reader from the fiction itself; it calls attention to the book as artifice and makes clear the reader's importance in creating that fiction; it allows the book to seem to be a book about itself. The narrator often reports crucial information to the reader that remains unknown to the novel's characters. For example, the narrator tells the reader that Miss Trowbridge "had married Mr. Pym without telling her guardian for fear he might refuse permission" (*Harry*, 16). The fact that other characters, especially Constable Narbut (who proposes to Miss Trowbridge and becomes angry at her refusal of him) and Harry (who mistrusts her mysterious visitor and begins to mistrust her as well), do not know about the marriage accelerates the plot. However, the reader must know about it in order to appreciate the story's ironic humor. "This is an invitation to farce, and farcical indeed is the web of misconstructions that follows, with hapless Harry as the dupe of Skatch and the remorseless accuser of innocent Miss Trowbridge" (Sutherland 1980, 46). In fact, this self-conscious narrator becomes merely a tool with which the author manipulates the plot and the tone of the novel.

Describing the novel as a comedy and its tone as ironic seems particularly curious given Avi's intention to compose "a grim, relentless tragedy about a kid whose fearfulness made him positively evil. There was not the slightest notion of anything funny."[14] The mask of tragedy becomes the mask of comedy as the pathetic, pampered Horatio (who must be named after Horatio Alger) develops into the confident hero Harry. His eavesdropping yields both good information and misinformation. Harry overhears Miss Trowbridge talk about the money box. Later, when he sees her embrace Mr. Pym, Harry decides the couple are thieves, and he pilfers the money box, hiding it in the chimney in his parents' bedroom. He holds the secret dearly and cleverly, even from the wily Skatch. When Skatch discovers the truth and traps him, Harry shows his resolve and his agility in climbing up the chimney onto the roof. Eventually, Harry lives up to the praises heaped upon him by Mr. Skatch; he proves himself to be a "decent, honest, pious" (*Harry*, 135) and "bold, brave boy" (*Harry*, 66).

Whereas Harry earns the description of hero first applied to him in chapter 1, Mr. Skatch, the peddler of religious books for children, emerges as the villain. Just as Emily Upham recited a poem from *Mrs. E. P. Miller's Mother Truth's Melodies: Common Sense for Children*, a popular book of poetry during the historical period of the novel's setting, so does Jeremiah Skatch sing the hymns and poems by the renowned children's poet Isaac Watts in *Divine Songs Attempted in Easy Language for the Use of Children*. Avi does not parody Watts's poems in the outrageously direct way that Lewis Carroll does in *Alice in Wonderland;* instead, he trusts his reader to realize the falseness of the song's singer. The songs and poems ironically point to Skatch's hypocrisy; untrustworthy, greedy, and perhaps murderous, Skatch calls for benevolence and love.

The novel's end finds Harry, like Emily, once again typecast by his family. In fact, Emily, Seth, and Harry all change when the parents are absent. As in many children's books, the parents are dismissed early in the novel (Emily is sent on a journey; Harry's parents take a trip). Yet, the didactic tracts and songs for children by adults underscore the oppressiveness of the adult world, a world that does not recognize, or perhaps cannot tolerate, the independence of children. In these two spoofs, Avi highlights adult hypocrisy as he celebrates the potential of children.

The early descriptions of Emily and Harry resemble Avi's depiction of himself as a child. He reports "being born a sickly child" whose father was largely absent working on a fellowship at Johns Hopkins University in Baltimore and whose mother seemed overwhelmed by caring for twins and an older toddler (interview). Like the parents of Emily and Harry, Avi's appear to have been somewhat removed. He describes himself not as an unhappy child but as an isolated one. He reports bonding with his twin sister

Emily, who was discovered early in life to have some sort of heart condition, and participating in the extended family life of his mother's sister.

These two books suggest that in the historical tension between teaching children and entertaining them, Avi, faulting didactic instruction, chooses to write stories that solicit fun and entertainment. Both books use broad descriptions that invoke humor. Avi crafts similes that not only crystallize description but that also add humor. The narrator describes Harry's father as "large. That is, he was too big for his stiff starched shirt, too big for his jacket, and too big for the side whiskers that stuck out from his round face like the bare wings of a plucked chicken" (*Harry*, 4). Paul O. Zelinsky's black-and-white pen drawings complement the text's attitude. By controlling hyperbole for the purpose of entertaining readers, they also turn dramatic moments into melodramatic ones.

Something Upstairs

The History of Helpless Harry ends as it began, with the narrator speaking directly to the reader. Remaining outside the story to characterize himself as the author, the narrator invites readers to let him know about other stories in need of telling. Avi adopts a similar, although more self-conscious, narrative stance in *Something Upstairs*. Rather than inserting the narrator's comments to the reader as a mechanism for relating the story and developing tone, Avi interjects himself as one of the novel's characters, as "the writer of books for kids, as someone who hears a story from a boy, Kenny Huldorf, and, with the boy's permission, tells his story. It is the story of a story" ("Seeing," 6). Avi maintains that he

> told the story this way . . . because I don't believe in ghosts. But I thought that if I told the story in terms of someone else's belief in ghosts it *would* have impact. I was right. It appears to be very convincing. Since the publication of the book I have been truly astonished by the number of people who believe it to be a true story, or even believe that aspects of the book are true. I am not

just speaking of kids. Many an adult has wanted to know what
parts of the tale are true. One indignant adult demanded that I
share my royalties with Kenny Huldorf. ("Seeing," 6)

Indeed, the novel works effectively as "a suspenseful tale of multiple hauntings, time travel, and murder in old Rhode Island."[15]

In *Something Upstairs,* Avi combines a number of stylistic genres. Initially, it opens as a realistic story about Kenny, a young
boy who wants to share an actual experience with an author visiting his school. Kenny's story begins in the present, with his move
from Los Angeles to Providence, Rhode Island, during the summer. Elements of historical fiction creep in as Kenny adjusts to
his new home in the historical Daniel Stillwell House, built in
1789. Kenny explores his renovated attic room and "recalls . . .
that a few nights after they moved in the heat had become so
awful it was particularly hard for him to fall asleep. And then
when he did, a mosquito awakened him. At least Kenny thought
it was a mosquito."[16]

This disturbance spurs speculation about the room's past occu-
pants, and Kenny begins to follow noises in the night, actions that
initiate the ghost story. In turn, the haunting of Kenny by Caleb,
a slave who lived and died in the attic room in 1800, becomes the
avenue for Kenny's time travel into the past. The precise, realistic details of Providence in 1800 sharpen the fantastic elements of
the ghost story and time travel; similarly, the factual descriptions
of Rhode Island in the late 1900s ground the novel in the present.
In telling a story with this temporal complexity, Avi expertly uses
verb tenses as a way of placing and moving the reader in and out
of multiple time frames. The present tense highlights Kenny's
recounting of the story to Avi; the past tense is Avi's writing of
Kenny's story about the past.

"Bored. Restless. Edgy" (*Upstairs,* 10) prove qualities that
make Kenny ripe for adventure. To fill his time, Kenny begins to
study Providence and its history. Like so many of Avi's characters—Chris in *No More Magic* and Andy in *Wolf Rider*—Kenny
asks questions as a way of learning.

Though he had never been particularly interested in history, Kenny now felt an urge to know about the old days. More than once he asked himself, Who were the people of this house? What did they look like? Did they wear funny suits, wigs, dresses? Were there any kids? How did they live? And, for that matter— how did they die? (*Upstairs*, 11)

Like Andy in *Wolf Rider*, Kenny's curiosity leads to a sense of responsibility and speculation about "a human death" (*Upstairs*, 10). Kenny's rather intellectual study materializes in the ghostly form of 16-year-old Caleb. Initially, Kenny sees Caleb, who runs from him, but eventually the two talk. Caleb slowly divulges to Kenny his history as a slave and his murder in the attic room. Mistrustful of Kenny but needing his help to gain release from his ghostliness, Caleb entreats Kenny to help find his murderer. Kenny's "distinct feeling of shock" (*Upstairs*, 39) at the request signals a tension between the two characters that persists nearly to the novel's end. Kenny is willing to help Caleb as long as he need assume only minimal risk. When his compassionate desire to help Caleb requires that he travel to the past, to haunt the past as Caleb does the present and to change the course of events in the past, Kenny is "torn between guilt and fearfulness" (*Something*, 60). Like Morwenna in *Bright Shadow*, who will die if she spends her last wish, Kenny fears losing himself in saving another. Caleb's rejection of Kenny's historical research as lies causes Kenny to ask deeper, more challenging, and less answerable questions. Believing Caleb, Kenny loses faith in historical documents, and the two forge a new bond built on mutual trust. Having mistakenly counted on others to free him from slavery and to rescue him from his past hauntings, Caleb now gambles on Kenny to help him solve the murder.

This shift in confidence launches Kenny's travel into the past and into Caleb's memory.

After a moment of hesitation Kenny reached toward him. And he has a distinct memory of their hands meeting. He saw that. He insists he felt nothing, no more than if he'd held his fingers to the air. But gradually Caleb did take on weight, form, and warmth, until their hands —hands of flesh and blood—were linked. (*Upstairs*, 67–68)

Kenny persists in holding on to his key chain as a link to his present. When Kenny realizes that the Pardon Willinghast, whom he knows as the historical librarian, actually lives in the past as a slave trader, he clings yet more tenaciously to the chain. Willinghast fosters Kenny's faith in the key chain's potential when he attempts to blackmail Kenny into killing Caleb. Perhaps the chain serves as a red herring. Kenny awakens in the present with the chain in his hand. However, is it taking the key chain from Willinghast that returns Kenny to the present? Or, more importantly, is Kenny able to reclaim his own life by shooting Willinghast, setting the past to rights, keeping his promises to Caleb, and freeing Caleb from slavery and death in 1800 and from the bondage of haunting the future?

Kenny awakens in his present to find that the floor's blood "stain was gone" (*Upstairs*, 117). Yet, because the narrative structure of the novel insists upon Kenny telling his story, readers know "how deeply troubled he was" (*Upstairs*, 120). Willinghast promises Kenny that he will feel no remorse at killing the slave Caleb, that "your memory will be your alibi" (*Upstairs*, 116). Kenny sees Caleb not as a slave but as an individual, a fact that makes it impossible to kill him. Ironically, Kenny's view of Willinghast as a human being, evil and despicable but human nonetheless, perpetuates his contrition at having murdered Willinghast. Even though the newspaper and gravestone declare the death a suicide, Kenny knows his guilt. Like Jonathan in *The Fighting Ground*, Kenny is haunted by his complicity, by his all-too-human ability to act cruelly. Wondering whether his journey into the past and his killing of Willinghast were worthwhile, Kenny concludes his confidence in Avi by asking if Caleb will ever be free. It is a query that appeals to Avi, the visiting author and storyteller who has the ability—by telling the story—to free Kenny from this tale, to discharge him back into his life without this burden.

Something Upstairs turns on various modes of imprisonment. Time holds first Caleb and then Kenny hostage. Caleb's memory becomes Kenny's jailer as the two must reenact the past to find a path to freedom. Willinghast's memory, too, attempts to fetter Kenny. In these ways, Avi explores "an extended metaphor of the notion that we are all haunted by our history" ("Seeing," 7). Yet, Avi intensifies that metaphor; history reaches beyond the personal accounts of these characters and back into a collective social and cultural record that continues to imprison us today. The novel exceeds being a "ghost story of redeeming social value"[17] to stand as a provocative extension of Avi's other books that raise questions about slavery, such as *Captain Grey, Encounter at Easton,* and *Night Journey.* In discussing this novel, Avi writes that "as far as our nation is concerned, issues of race and racism are paramount. No other problem is as fundamental to our past, our present, our future. . . . I [believe] the problem of racism is so crucial. Which is why I wrote the book and tell the story" ("Seeing," 6–7).

The narrative framework "told as the author heard it from the main character, adds a dimension of eerie reality to this tale of ghosts, time travel, slavery, and murder that will satisfy the most avid adventure reader."[18] However, it also contributes an essential element of metafiction.

> *Metafiction* is a term given to fictional writing which self-consciously and systematically draws attention to its status as artefact in order to pose questions about the relationship between fiction and reality.[19]

The Man Who Was Poe

In *The Man Who Was Poe* Avi imagines the writer Edgar Allan Poe as an author, as a historical person, and as a fictional character. Avi exploits Poe's occupation as a writer to consider the relationship between fiction and reality. Calling himself Auguste Dupin, Poe meets 11-year-old Edmund, who searches desperately for his missing twin sister, Sis, and his aunt Pru. Dupin/Poe

agrees to help Edmund partly because he sees the fictional potential in Edmund's situation. " 'Is there,' he began, 'a story to be
made out of this boy's circumstances?' "[20] As the novel progresses, Dupin/Poe tries to write reality—or, as Edmund believes,
tries to make reality into the fiction he has conceived.

Avi has the character Poe take on the name of the author Poe's
character Dupin, the ingenious detective in the Parisian mysteries,
including "Murders at the Rue Morgue." This intertextuality causes
a circular self-reference; a referentiality controlled by Avi the
author similar to the ways in which Dupin wants to control his narrative. Once Poe takes on the name Dupin, he finds himself actually
being Dupin, the solver of mysteries. However, because Avi makes
clear Dupin's actual identity as Poe, the character maintains his life
as a creator of fiction even as he actively works to solve Edmund's
mystery. If Poe the writer could craft the mystery story, then his
alter ego Dupin could solve it. Of course, Dupin remains a character,
which makes Poe a character, in a book by Avi.

Avi the author cautions his readers to "never fully trust the
author, never fully trust my characters, never fully trust my
story, no, not even my words. Above all, when you finish the story
and come to a conclusion that you know what it means, it's crucial never to assume that *I* know what it means. . . . Good *writing*,
I think, comes about when the writer's conscious mastery of technique allows his or her unconscious to be revealed" ("Seeing,"
3–4). These words and the stories told by Avi and by the
author/character Dupin/Poe suggest that authors alone do not
control their stories. In that sense, then, this novel pushes the
conventions of metafiction.

> [A] fully self-conscious novel . . . is one in which from beginning
> to end, through the style, the handling of narrative viewpoint,
> the names and words imposed on the characters, the patterning
> of the narration, the nature of the characters and what befalls
> them, there is a consistent effort to convey to us a sense of the
> fictional world as an authorial construct.[21]

The "to us" in the passage extends the creative role of fiction and
metafiction from the author to the reader. As Avi demonstrates

fictionally through the character of Dupin/Poe, as the writer embarks on the novel, he attempts to impart to the reader his awareness of the nature of language. Dupin/Poe becomes agitated when Edmund insists on finding his sister rather than trusting that Dupin/Poe will write their ending. Edmund acts as an unreliable reader, a reader unwilling to participate in the construction of Dupin's/Poe's fiction. The reader, then, recognizes that the words of the novel generate meaning *but within* the confines of the novel itself; Edmund insists that the "real" ending of his search for Sis will not follow Dupin's/Poe's fictional conclusion. To enter the novel *The Man Who Was Poe* is to participate in a world informed by the novel's condition as fiction and to explore the limitations and possibilities that condition embodies.

Like the predecessors of Andy in *Wolf Rider* and Kenny in *Something Upstairs*, Dupin/Poe often thinks of death. Like Morwenna in *Bright Shadow*, his obsessive thoughts about death lead one to realize that it is his own dying that he fears most. Yet, in adopting the persona of Dupin, who seeks to unravel death, Poe relinquishes his own identity, a demise of sorts. For Dupin/Poe, his story's ending directs the story itself. As he outlines ideas for a story about Edmund, Dupin/Poe thinks: "Why must death always be certain? Could he never escape it? Never think of another ending?" (*Poe*, 32) Edmund's tenacious conviction that his sister lives presents Dupin/Poe with other possible endings; however, his inability to imagine these alternatives risks channeling this story down its inevitable path.

Avi's contrast of Dupin/Poe, the alcoholic, demon-possessed writer who can envision only death as an ending, with Edmund, who clings expectantly to life, charges readers to "create meaning out of the apparent chaos" ("Seeing," 4). Edmund's life fixation allows him to see that Dupin/Poe does not fear dying, rather "it's living [he's] frightened of" (*Poe*, 205). Living, unlike fiction, remains unfinished and incomplete. Although Poe suggests that characters live eternally in fiction, Edmund understands the separation between fiction and reality. Edmund, as the novel's insistent call to reality and to life, destroys Poe's manuscript, leaving only its opening paragraph. The novel ends with Edmund reading the opening of Poe's story, which is also the opening of Avi's novel *The Man Who Was Poe*. Ultimately, Avi asserts not the actual reality but the fiction's ties to reality and celebrates fiction as an author's construction that transforms life's "confusion, disorder" ("Seeing," 4) into a controlled order, a story with a beginning, a middle, and an end.

At the moment when Dupin reveals himself as the "great writer" Poe, he tells Edmund that "[l]ies have their own truth" (*Poe*, 149). Poe thus alludes to the falsity of fiction, which is "a mask with the eye holes placed—by the writer—in such a way that the reader notices only certain things" ("Seeing," 4). Avi comments on fiction in his fiction, reminding readers of the boundaries between the fictional world and the real world. Fiction is not the real world presented in truth; rather, it is the "best way of approaching truth" ("Seeing," 4) because it invites readers' questions and provokes their individual answers.

Reviewers describe the book as "a complex, atmospheric thriller,"[22] an "intriguing, absorbing, and carefully, logically, and intricately plotted"[23] mystery. One might contend that the most terrifying aspects of this work reside in its metafictional questions. Through this book, Avi asks challenging, disturbing questions about the nature of illusion and reality, about the relationship between life and fiction. At a party at the home of his intended wife, Mrs. Helen Whitman, Poe discusses his poetry and fiction with other guests. They share with him how uncomfortable, how "low, bestial, sordid" (*Poe*, 124) they find his fiction. Later, Poe articulates that his "art is too strong. I frighten the timid" (*Poe*, 204). It seems that both Poe and Avi would contend that the function of art is to disturb, to present the uncomfortable, to be strong in its challenge. Of course, other considerations of Avi's work in this book suggest that Avi would also embrace the ability of art to evoke laughter as well as pain, to delight as well as instruct, to entertain even as it might disturb.

Avi talks about

the origins of this story in this way: "Poe is an incredible and complex figure who's absolutely adored by many young people.

What happens if you confront him—this crazy, alcoholic, weird, brilliant man—with a kid? That's a historical question, but after that, it's about the relationship, not about history or the moment in history."[24]

Poe figures in an early version of Avi's *Something Upstairs.* Returning to several different historical times, Kenny and Caleb meet Poe on a time-travel journey. Although Avi deleted any reference to times other than 1800 in his final manuscript of *Something Upstairs*, he saw his speculations about Poe leading to another book. Indeed, Avi himself was unaware that 84 Benefit Street, the address of Mrs. Helen Whitman's actual home, appears in both *Something Upstairs* and *The Man Who Was Poe.* Once again history serves as backdrop. Avi includes precise details about the shipping port of Providence, Rhode Island, of 1848 even as he shrouds the story in the fogginess of mystery. The descriptions of the docks, the clothing, the crowded cafes, and the legal proceedings fill out the setting. The claustrophobic living quarters of the poor immigrant Edmund contrast sharply with the expansive grounds, the lush clothing, and the general luxury of the upper-class Whitman family living in downtown Providence.

History provides the setting, and, to a degree, it dictates the character of Dupin/Poe. However, as Avi suggests above, this story also succeeds because it has a historical appeal. Edmund, lonely and timid, has clear motivation to seek his only personal connection to the world, his twin sister, Sis. For the brief time during which readers see Sis, they come to know her as thoughtful and clever. Like Gretel from her favorite fairy tale, Sis leaves pearl buttons as a path to her discovery. Sis's abduction imparts a remarkably "Dickensian flavor" (Watson, 205) to the mystery through the meanderings of its intricate plot and sustained suspense.

A seemingly small, unimportant historical ingredient takes on multifaceted significance in this novel. Mrs. Helen Whitman asks Poe to have a daguerreotype taken of himself to give to her. The guests at her party have difficulty reconciling Poe's ordinary face

with the sinister, dark side expressed in his art. Mrs. Whitman
wants this fixed portrait of him "to study [his] character at . . .
leisure" (*Poe*, 125). Historically, the daguerreotype represents the
newest technology in portraiture. In terms of plot, Poe sees a
daguerreotype of Edmund's mother and believes her to be alive
and in Providence. That fact helps to solve the mystery because
Poe realizes that he has not been haunted by the ghost of dead
Aunt Pru but that her twin sister, Edmund's mother, still lives
and is in Providence, searching for her children and seeking a
divorce from her diabolical husband, Ratchett. Metaphorically,
the daguerreotype underscores the novel's tensions between masquerade and identity, between illusion and reality. Edmund asks
Poe

> "What did that daguerreotype tell you?" . . . "I don't under-
> stand anything you say to me! You treat me well and then you
> speak and do awful things. I don't even know who you are or
> what your name is." (*Poe*, 145)

Dupin's true identity as Poe cannot be revealed by the daguerreotype; instead, he will unmask himself as Poe only when he no
longer wants to follow the mystery but rather feels capable of fin-
ishing his story. He names himself as "writer, not adventurer. My
function is to think. And then to write about what I think. . . . I
am no longer concerned with *your* story. As for *my* story, I have a
more elaborate ending to pursue. . . . I'm no longer Auguste
Dupin. I am the man who *is* Edgar—Allan—Poe" (*Poe*, 168). In
asserting his identity, Dupin claims his role as the creator of illusion. Like fiction, a daguerreotype captures only an image of reality. Art, too, can only mirror reality through an illusion. Mrs.
Whitman wants to examine Poe's daguerreotype to learn truth
from the image, an illusion. In contrast, Poe "studied [Edmund's]
face. Now he was no longer certain it was his character" (*Poe*,
179). Unable to reconcile the actual Edmund with his character,
Poe wants illusion to dictate reality.

Avi's concluding biographical note about "the man who was
Poe" touches again on some of these questions. This short biogra-

phy cannot be complete; therefore, like fiction, it takes its strength from its selectivity. Avi tells not the whole truth about Poe but shares the facts that are important to an understanding of this story. Story develops from reality. Does the biography present Poe as man, or does it reinforce comprehending Poe as a character in Avi's story? Or perhaps the reverse is true: Does the novel create the character of Dupin/Poe as a way of better "approaching truth" ("Seeing," 4) about the man who was Poe as presented in the epilogue? For readers unfamiliar with Poe as a literary figure, the postscript offers an opportunity for a different, more complex reading of the novel in which Poe functions both as character and as historical personage. The postscript alleges to separate the facts about Poe from Avi's fiction about him. However, the circle closes again as one recognizes that the selection of facts itself builds yet another fiction.

5. Avi as Risk-Taker

"What is the use of a book," thought Alice, "without pictures or conversations?"

—Lewis Carroll[1]

The physical appearance of a book, its design, and the placement of words and images on its pages influence the way in which the book is read; they also influence its readers and, ultimately, can even shape the story being told. In *City of Light, City of Dark, Who Was That Masked Man, Anyway?,* and *Nothing but the Truth,* Avi fuses form and content by merging narrative style with three distinctive styles of presentation.

City of Light, City of Dark

City of Light, City of Dark bears the subtitle "A Comic-Book Novel" and sports full black-and-white, pen-and-India-ink strip art by Brian Floca. An avid reader of comic books as a young boy, Avi here "uses a comic-book format to tell a comic-book tale about the forces of good and evil battling above, below, and upon the island of Manhattan."[2] The double-page spread that serves as title page immediately invokes a classic feature of the comic book: The illustration shows the recognizable geography and landmarks of Manhattan yet is labeled "Island of the Kurbs." Thus, the illustration claims the dual realistic and fantastic settings characteristic of comic books. Moreover, in its use of cartoon balloons to identify significant places in the story, this opening page establishes the codependency of art and text as storytelling mechanisms. Later, the balloons encapsulate dialogue and advance the action. At various points in the text, these bubbles work as effective mechanisms to include English translations of the Spanish spoken at one character's home.

The opening pages of the comic-book novel extend the Gothamesque nature of the tale. The two-dimensional art sharply contrasts a deep, flat ink-black line or shape against a stark, glossy white. Similarly, the story emphasizes with hyperbolic intensity the battle between light and dark, between good and evil. The Kurbs act as a dark, oppressive weight over the city; they threaten absolute evil if not appeased. Floca depicts the most evil character, Thor Underton, as a solid black shape moving heavily, deliberately through the pages. In comparison, the sources of good are defined by an economical, dynamic line; a snow-white brightness infuses their pages.

In addition to the horizontal strip art of the comic book, Floca improvises with vertical, sometimes diagonal, and occasionally panoramic perspectives to capture the activity demanded in the story. For example, when one character walks through Grand Central Station, the art stays horizontal; as that character moves into an underground search, the vertical strips impart a tunneling effect.[3] That same page begins by showing a smallish character entering the immense train station; however, as the action increasingly focuses on that character and the importance of his movements, the art zooms in to center eventually on the character's hand and its knocking motion. A similar dramatic effect is achieved later in the story. As the Kurbs carry away the wholly evil Underton, Floca starts with an aerial view, then shifts to ground level, where we see Underton's feet slowly being lifted. The final element of this scene places the reader in a slanted, midair position, looking not only down and left at the street-level character but also up and right at the captured Underton (*City*, 40–41). In this largely wordless, double-page spread, the visual layout enhances the dramatic drive of the story even as the artist pushes the action toward the right, off the page and into the next one. Art and text collaborate in this page-turning effect.

In addition to depicting the action of the story, Floca also inflects the tone. Crowded pages, pointed, triangular shapes, jagged lines, and frequent vanishing points highlight the story's energetic, nearly frantic, mystery. Juxtaposing the crude plane—built by the young boys and flown by magic—against the architectural sophistication of the Chrysler Building, the illustrations capture the sensational fantasy of flight (*City*, 152–53). Visual moments like these surprise and delight the reader.

Comic-book convention relies on surprise in plot and situation yet depends upon the recognizability of characters. The opening pages state clearly the contrivances of this story's plot as they define the Kurbs, their control of the Power to keep the city warm and safe, their contract and rules. The "Ritual Cycle of Acknowledgment" presents the deadlines that push the story and preserve the recognizable seasonal movement from winter to spring. Similarly, the responsibility of power passes from a chosen woman to her daughter. The opening pages provide readers with the requisite history to understand the events about to take place. With this information, the reader's motivation becomes not resolution to *what* will happen but discovery of *how* it will happen. The comic book outlines plot even as it holds back revealing details.

One reads comic books for their stories about unchanging, familiar characters. In this comic-book novel, the two-dimensional art anticipates the necessary flatness of the characters. Floca's line softens to depict the story's heroes. Readers can count on Carlos as the boy-hero from the moment they meet him. He proves himself trustworthy and diligent. Avi imbues Carlos with an inventiveness that he himself exercised as a child. *Popular Science* fascinates Carlos as it did Avi, and nourishes the boy's imagination, which leads to the invention of the rooftop airplane. Avi describes himself as less interested in science per se but rather more compelled by the intersection of science with "a Tom Swift myth."[4] Carlos becomes the Tom Swift character in this comic-book novel. And, like every true superhero, Carlos has his reliable sidekick—Tom.

Unlike *The Man Who Was Poe*, where the absent women are ever present, the women in this story constitute the nucleus of action: They are the heroes. The girl-hero Sarah commands greater significance than does Carlos. At first meeting, Sarah/ Estella is loyal, courageous, and smart. She obeys her father and acts only in ways supportive of him. As she unravels the mystery about the token, Sarah finds her mother, learns her own true name (Estella), and assumes the power and the role of Token Searcher. Yet, even at the story's end, readers believe in Estella's schoolgirl ordinariness. In contrast to her mother, Asterel, Estella puts personal obligations above public ones. Asterel acts responsibly in her role as Token Searcher; even when "faced [with] a terrible decision: should she complete the ritual of the token or set off to search for her baby . . . [s]he felt she had no choice. She must save the city" (*City*, 24). When forced to choose between returning the token or saving her father, Estella decides to save her father first. In true comic-book fashion, however, Estella manages to have it both ways: She saves her father *and* meets the Kurbs' deadline.

Embracing her new name and knowledge of her mother, Sarah/ Estella appears to change. Similarly, now anointed with the "searcher's gift of sight" (*City*, 21) passed matrilinearly from Asterel to her, Estella commands tremendous power. The visionary control imparted by the token shifts from the object and whoever holds it to Estella alone. With the power, Estella inherits the yearly obligation to complete the Ritual Cycle of Acknowledgment on the winter solstice. However, the comic-book novel's final images of Estella reinforce her stability: The book opens with domestic scenes of Sarah with her father and closes with similar scenes of Estella with her mother. She resumes an ordinary, regular life as she maintains her characteristic loyalty, strength, and intelligence.

Theo, who takes on the name Stubbs in an attempt to escape Underton, serves as foil to Asterel. Where she acts out of public responsibility and with determination, he submits and follows Underton. Although he creates a safe, reliable home for Sarah for eleven years, Theo/Stubbs complies when Underton requires her services. Unlike other characters whose allegiance with the good or evil forces in the story are immediately apparent, Theo/Stubbs

seems neither good nor evil. He lacks the strength to follow consistently his desire to do good; simultaneously, his basic decency
prevents him from succumbing to evil. In this way, Theo/Stubbs
also functions as foil to Thor Underton.

In contrast to Theo's/Stubbs's complacency, Thor Underton is a
single-minded zealot. Initially obsessed with the power to light
the neon creations that celebrate his name and his scientific
achievements, he becomes obsessed with the Kurbs' Power as the
only sufficient energy source to light his sign. Purely evil, Underton has a hard-edged face. He walks with a cane and is depicted as
a massive black shape moving through the city. Blinded by a stray
sliver of glass as Asterel destroys his masterwork "in rage and
panic" (*City*, 22) against his blackmail, Underton loses all
vision—the ability to see his own creations and the ability to
imagine anything except holding the Power. He no longer needs
the power to supply his creations but believes it can restore his
sight. His obsessions become increasingly self-focused; he will
willingly sacrifice the entire city for a moment of vision. Lacking
Theo's compassion for individuals, for humanity, he is ready to
enslave all others for his own benefit. In another broad comic-
book stroke, this evil force falls from the torch-platform of the
Statue of Liberty in his battle with good. The would-be enslaver
plunges from the national symbol of freedom.

Reviews of *City of Light, City of Dark* celebrate its "multicultural cast" (Sutton), which replicates present-day Manhattan. By
naming as heroes the African American Asterel and Estella and
the Latino Carlos and by identifying as evil the white Thor
Underton, the story invites readers to redefine the literary stereotypes that align good with light and evil with dark. Reviews of
this book describe it as one in Avi's "series of experiments in children's fiction."[5] In the context of Avi's entire body of work, this
novel seems less experimental and more like an exploration of different storytelling modes. Just as *Emily Upham's Revenge* and
The History of Helpless Harry drew on the conventions of Victorian melodrama, so does this comic-book novel exploit the reliable
expectations of comic-book reading as fundamental to its story,
its characters, its theme, and its telling. The final image of this

comic-book novel is conveyed by these words on an open book: "If Winter comes, can Spring be far behind?" (*City*, 192) This line from Shelley's poem "Ode to the West Wind" pulls the reader out of the comic-book mode and into the realm of classical poetry and literature. Thus, *City of Light, City of Dark* itself becomes a Ritual Cycle of Acknowledgment in which Avi, the reader developed by comic books, becomes the writer knowingly exploring—and paying homage to—the literary force of the comic book.

"Who Was That Masked Man, Anyway?"

According to one review, "Avi crafts another stylistic risk-taker [that] . . . juxtaposes actual radio programs from the 1940s with conversations between sixth-grader Frankie Wattleson and his parents, older brother, teacher, and neighbor."[6] Avi asserts that this is his only truly innovative novel. Although other comic-book novels, such as Art Spiegelman's *Maus*, had been written prior to *City of Light, City of Dark*, Avi believes that no other novel constructed of unattributed dialogue has been written. Whereas other novels may include signals to the reader—such as "he said" and "she asked"—no such markers identify the speakers in this novel. At the suggestion of his editor, Richard Jackson, Avi decided to tell this story solely in dialogue. Given these circumstances, form came before content, although the novel itself blends the two. The book may well be an "experiment in fiction"[7]; however, readers should avoid minimizing its achievement, authenticity, and originality.

Like *City of Light, City of Dark*, this novel draws upon Avi's childhood. He describes childhood pleasures that figure in his writing: reading comic books as well as serial novels such as Tom Swift, the Hardy Boys, and Westerns and listening intently to radio programs. Avi compares the relationship between Frankie and his neighbor Mario to his own relationship with his slightly younger cousin, Michael; the fictional characters reenact their form of play. Avi recalls first telling stories to Michael, whose house around the corner was Avi's second home.

Animation and dialogue typify children's play. They talk with one another and attribute dialogue to each other and to inanimate objects. In the novel, Frankie sets dialogue and animation in motion. Pulling Mario in as participant and as audience, Frankie dictates Mario's lines and directs his actions; as Frankie narrates the adventures of Chet Barker—Master Spy (his key role)—and Chet's reliable sidekick—Skipper O'Malley (Mario's role)—he advances their fictional adventures through dialogue.

> "I say, 'Thanks for saving my life, pardner. I can scramble on my own now.' You say, 'Tweren't nothing.' "
> "Tweren't nothing."
> "I say, 'The coast is clear.' I reach up and try the trapdoor. It opens slowly. Eerie organ music. Echo of feet on stone floor. Sound of water dripping. You look around with big eyes and say, 'Mighty creepy in here, Chet.' "
> "Mighty creepy in here, Chet."[8]

Frankie creates the dialogue he and Mario speak to each other; in turn, that dialogue establishes the characters the boys will act out. Through dialogue Frankie—and, ultimately Avi—not only conveys characters in action but also develops atmosphere and establishes physical and temporal settings. On those few occasions when Mario questions Frankie's story-in-progress, Frankie answers hastily and reclaims control of his script.

The boys' playacting straddles the line between fiction and reality. Mario maintains the ability to distinguish between the two and often enlightens Frankie on life's truths. Frankie, however, has difficulty differentiating between fiction and reality. Consumed by radio programs, he derives his play from the airwaves. His stories echo the adventures of the Lone Ranger, the Green Hornet, Buck Rogers, the Shadow, and other costumed heroes of the wireless. Even when asked to read from a basal reader at school, Frankie leaves the written text to indulge his own stories. By incorporating the radio programs into the lives of its characters, the novel's dialogue format becomes one extended script, thereby dissolving the distinction between radio and life. Frankie, however, remains unable to make that discrimination. He approaches life as if it were a series of heroic episodes with only modest commercial interruptions for school and family obligations.

Frankie reduces people to the stereotypes easily recognized from radio dramas. His brother Tom, returning from the war, becomes his hero, whereas Mr. Swerdlow, the boarder whom he considers intrusive, Frankie casts as villain. As a result, Frankie undertakes adventures to celebrate Tom's heroism—and win him the girl—and to rid his family of Mr. Swerdlow. Readers recognize Frankie's plot as comedy—even farce—because they know what he will not admit: that he cannot script others' lives to fit his intended ending. A remarkable egocentrism underlies all of Frankie's inventions. At times Frankie silences Mario because he desires an audience, not a sidekick; Frankie's escapades to marry off Tom and eliminate Mr. Swerdlow stem largely from his wish to have his room and radio back again, to be across the alley again from Mario and his radio.

Three other elements factor into Frankie's obsession with radio programs and his own heroic adventures. Intelligent and creative, Frankie finds life, especially school, downright boring and unchallenging. Just as war movies did, the radio programs offered a country at war romanticized versions of a harsher reality; in contrast to the brutal scenes on the newsreels, they entertained those at home with visions of brave soldiers. The fiction Frankie speaks sometimes betrays the world he denies. He opens one of his adventures with "in a troubled, confused, mixed-up, twisted, and also puzzled world" (*Masked*, 108). This description reveals the reality of America during World War II, an existence that Frankie rejects as he insists upon transforming what he sees into something more glamorous. Frankie dismisses Mario's description of the world and offers his own:

> "Okay. What do you see over there?"
> "On the street?"
> "Yeah. What do you see?"
> "The street. Houses. Windows. Doors. And people. Cars. And the mailman coming."
> "Naw. That's the way grown-ups see. You want to know what I can see?"

"What?"

"One of those cars is a disguised rocket car. And behind that window—with the service star—there's a genius inventor. And that person walking there has a secret identity. And it could be the mailman is really a G-man, or even Doctor Oddball, and in his bag he's got an Instant Radio Double Relay Spy Noticer."

"You don't *know* any of that."

"So what? Everything would be better that way, wouldn't it?" (*Masked*, 114–15)

Clearly, Frankie beholds both worlds. He actively rejects the "real" world as adults see it and opts instead for the improvements offered by a child's unrestrained imagination. Not caring if he gets held back a year in school, wanting the room in which he grew up, and clinging to a child's view of the world, Frankie resists maturing.

Why does Frankie resist growing up? Because doing so would require that he relinquish the fantasies he conjures up to deal with daily life. Growing up would mean discarding his faith in heroes, even acknowledging his "heroic" brother Tom as a vulnerable, frightened, cowardly, and lucky soldier.

Like any writer of fiction, Frankie creates a world that he can control. In telling stories, he can extract order out of the chaos he sees. Avi draws the parallel most clearly when he asserts that "when I write comedy I am closest to the person I was as a child in Brooklyn, New York: fighting off impending disaster, profound pessimism and authority with irony and sarcasm, all with a deliberate fog of confusion". If Frankie, like the writer, creates the confusion, then he also controls it. And to control it is to understand it.

The escalation of Frankie's plot to introduce his brother to his teacher, Miss Gomez, whose boyfriend has been killed in the war, confronts Frankie the writer with Frankie the realist. Frankie orchestrates a meeting between his brother and his teacher by lying to his mother to get her out of the house. However, when Tom confronts Frankie with the truth about his war experience, Frankie no longer wants to execute the plan; he believes "it's a mistake" (*Masked*, 157) and wants to get out of it. Here, Frankie alters his control over the situation. Rather than reach for the happy ending, Frankie tries to prevent the embarrassment he believes will occur if Tom and Miss Gomez meet. Therefore, he tries to undo what he has set up to happen. Ironically, the more he tries to reverse the course of events, to help his brother escape out the window via the plank that connects him to Mario's room, the more events elude his control. The fiction takes on a life of its own, a comedy that reduces Tom and Miss Gomez—and the reader—to laughter. This scene provides comic relief to Frankie and to readers after Tom's tragic confession to Frankie. And, like Tom's confession, Frankie learns that even that which is out of his control can be appreciated and understood.

The book's final scene puts Frankie back in action, spying on his brother's wedding night activities and asserting his faith in radio as he writes the closing piece. Because he listens rather than speaks, Frankie's hyperbolic voice loses a measure of intensity here. Furthermore, the scene depicts a subtle shift from Frankie as the sole believer in imaginative powers when the new Mrs. Wattleson recounts to her husband an "extraordinary" vision.

"The ultimate effect [of the novel] is paradox: readers can close their eyes and listen."[9] The effect is paradoxical also because Avi's exclusive use of dialogue places readers outside the novel: They can read and listen, just as Frankie can only listen to his radio programs. Yet, from that position, they can question, too. Readers know more about the story and other characters than Frankie does, which enables them to observe the satire in Frankie's comedy. Even as Avi lauds the storytelling power of the radio, he also "mocks [the] heroic stereotypes"[10] it presents, suggests the disappointment caused by its more commercial aspects, and questions "the mesmerizing effects of the media."[11]

Nothing but the Truth

Nothing but the Truth extends this discussion. Flipping the mask of comedy to that of tragedy, this "documentary novel" interrogates the nature of heroism as it "prods and provokes readers to question facts, behavior, and motivations."[12] Avi presents information from a variety of sources: newspapers and radio, school administration policies, political speeches, conversations between families and friends, even diaries, letters, and memoranda. Avi reports that "Living Newspapers," a type of theater in the 1930s that used dialogue and document readings, inspired the structure of this novel.[13] Because no single narrator tells the story, no single character's viewpoint directs it. Reviews of the novel found this "construction . . . nearly flawless"[14] and essential to the book's thematic intention. Avi considers that

> what is unusual about this book . . . is that there is no *visible* narration. . . . The story is revealed through an accumulation of documents. . . . These fragments are set out in chronological order but each document is independent of the other. It is the reader—and *only* the reader—who has all this information before him or her. It is the reader and only the reader who connects the documents—who draws the dots, so to speak—so that a picture is created. ("Seeing," 7)

Absence of visible narration does not mean complete lack of narration. In fact, Avi structures the book with absolute authorial control, a command that entices readers to believe that "the author's voice. . . . *appears* to have been banished from every page" ("Seeing," 7). However, these characters, events, and documents stem from Avi's imagination. *Nothing but the Truth* operates solely within Avi's fictional world. Even though subtitled as a documentary novel, all material presented stems from the author's imagination. Unlike film documentaries that collect facts, all information in this novel is created by Avi; "because the book takes enormous pains to deny the author's hand, it should alert [the reader] that [the author's] hand is *everywhere*" ("Seeing," 7). Like the director of a film documentary, Avi orders the presentation; he chooses where to allow gaps; he assembles the fictional material and presents it as fact.

What point of view does Avi's invisible narration promote? A combined point of view; "at least two people are required to experience literature completely: the writer *and* the reader" ("Seeing," 3). Although this pairing seems essential to any work of fiction, *Nothing but the Truth* makes explicit the interaction between the fiction (writer) and the reader. This novel demands that readers formulate a narrative bias of their own. Moreover, Avi's ordered presentation of the documents "[keeps] his audience unsettled"[15] as it forces them to continually redefine their perspectives, their alliances, and their allegiances when given new information.

The novel begins with an introduction of theme, rather than of character. Two questions precede page one: "Do you swear to tell the truth, the whole truth, and nothing but the truth? Does anyone say no?"[16] Not only does the first question repeat the title of the book, but also it invokes the legal system. The second question immediately causes readers to wonder why no one says "no." "If someone said they would not tell the truth in court, we *would* believe them" ("Seeing," 7). Yet, risking being found in contempt of court, everyone says "yes" without thought, even without option. "In short, we are all required to lie even as we swear to tell the truth" ("Seeing," 7). These two questions plunge readers immediately into the thematic depths of the novel: Truth is elusive; the truthteller, unreliable; and the system, corrupt.

Bearing the school district's letterhead, page one outlines the fill-in-the-blank guidelines for all school morning announcements. This is the only document presented out of chronological order and without reference to a specific date. As a document, the memo serves as a template for morning announcements; as a storytelling device, it identifies the pattern that, once broken, launches the plot. This form-memo appears once in the novel, yet knowledge of the order of events it prescribes becomes key to interpreting the story, as various settings and characters deviate from this norm. For example, the script outlined by the memo can be detected in the first part of chapter 2, set in Bernard Lunser's homeroom class. The departures from the script are more important, however. The teacher cracks jokes and makes fun of the announcements, the school, and the students. His attitude conveys nothing but a coy disrespect for the speaker, the school principal, Dr. Gertrude Doane, and for the process itself. Lunser does not sing the national anthem, he talks through it. The chapter introduces Philip Malloy, whom Lunser mocks for studying quietly during the anthem. Despite the fact that the memo calls for silence, the chapter calls that morning in Lunser's homeroom a "discussion" (*Truth*, 6).

The second homeroom discussion occurs in Margaret Narwin's class. She attempts to sort out the chaos caused by reassigning students to new homerooms. Despite the initial confusion, Narwin quiets the class to listen to the morning program. In contrast to Lunser, she attends to the morning announcements quietly as asked. Therefore, readers, like Narwin, instantly note Philip's digression from the expected procedure. Philip does not cease humming when first asked to by Narwin; when asked a third time, he states that he is "just humming" (*Truth*, 35), and by the fourth request the student and teacher are pitted against one another. The scene depicts the teacher performing her duties and the student continuing to act in ways that other teachers have considered appropriate. Neither party does anything wrong, except the lines of authority that can prevent genuine communications have been drawn. The next chapter shows the same setting on the following day. This time only Narwin's voice is heard. Philip does not answer her questions and she becomes more directive. She concludes the scene by exercising her authority to send Philip to the assistant principal's office for reprimand.

By the third day, the exchange has escalated to an altercation. She recognizes his voice and asks him explicitly to stop singing. This teacher tries to educate, not just teach (as the school motto proclaims) when she tells Philip the reason this behavior must stop: "Your actions are thoroughly disrespectful" (*Truth*, 59). Philip shows adolescent courage as he claims his right to sing; more disturbing, however, is Philip's audacity when he retorts, "It's you who's being disrespectful!" (*Truth*, 60) Whereas the first comment challenges Narwin's authority, the second attacks her personally. This shift anticipates two strands of truth that define the novel: the authoritative truth that binds a society versus the personal truth of an individual.

Avi furnishes the novel with material revealing a personal side to Philip and to Narwin. Readers learn about Philip through his diary, his conversations with his parents, and with his friends; they learn about Narwin through letters to her sister, conversations with her sister and others, and memos sent to her by Dr. Doane, her principal. Yet even these cannot be trusted to evidence a truthful side to a character. Philip's diaries bespeak his passion for track, yet some conversations with his father betray that passion. Philip writes in early diary entries with spirit, enthusiasm, and confidence. He expresses typical adolescent concerns (and assumptions) about male-female relationships, about school, and about family. His diary entries midway through the novel reveal doubt about his actions with Narwin and stretch to affirm his "rightness." His later entries describe his nervousness about returning to school after his expulsion for disobedience to Narwin; they also divulge his idea of approaching Narwin and disclose a weak optimism about setting right the terribly wrong course of events. His final entry abandons all hope and reveals only a defeated, self-consumed boy.

Putting the diary in the tight chronology with which Avi structures the book also places it within the context of plot events. At the beginning of the novel, Philip is merely another kid at school, although his diary celebrates his uniqueness, his "Malloy Magic" (*Truth*, 3). Ironically, the novel's ending finds Philip a patriotic hero whereas his diary illustrates his fall. What accounts for the change in Philip? He shares with his parents information about what has happened in school, but he also keeps information from them. Philip alternately wants to be like his father, the track star, and revolts against emulating him. He cannot face telling his parents that his poor grade in English removes him from the track team nor does he tell them that the cause of his grade is his poor performance in English. By extension, Philip does not tell the whole truth when he is suspended from school. Rather than honestly describe his relationship with Narwin, the English teacher who has failed him and, therefore, prevented him from participating in track, Philip simply asserts that the teacher has it out for him.

Even though Philip's partial facts preclude his parents from knowing him truly, they also result from Philip's not knowing his parents well. His father struggles at work, and, although eager for his father's support, Philip wants his father only to think well of him. His mother also works to maintain the family. She resents being called from work to pick him up after his suspension. The family gets so caught up in superficialities and details, truths that seem minor in context of the entire novel, that they cannot listen thoroughly.

7:12 P.M.
Discussion
between Philip Malloy and His Parents
During Dinner

Mr. Malloy: Okay, Phil. Now, I want to hear the whole thing. Start to finish. Just understand, right from the start, we're on your side. We don't intend to just take it. But I have to know what happened. Go on now.

Philip Malloy: Same as before.

Mr. Malloy: Same as *what* before?

Mrs. Malloy: He's trying to tell you dear.

Philip Malloy: See, they play "The Star-Spangled Banner" at the beginning of school. . . .

Mr. Malloy: I understand. When I was a kid we pledged allegiance. Go on.

Philip Malloy: A tape.

Mr. Malloy: Okay.

Philip Malloy: When—before—when I was in Mr. Lunser's class, he was like, almost asking me to sing out loud.

Mrs. Malloy: I always thought Philip had a good voice.

Mr. Malloy: That's not exactly relevant! Go on.

Philip Malloy: But this teacher—

Mr. Malloy: Mrs. Narwin.

Philip Malloy: It's Miss.

Mr. Malloy: Figures.

Mrs. Malloy: That has nothing to do with it, Ben!

Mr. Malloy: Go on.

Philip Malloy: She won't let me. Threw me out of class.

Mrs. Malloy: The principal said it was a rule.

Philip Malloy: Ma, he's the *assistant* principal.

Mr. Malloy: But why does that mean suspension?

Philip Malloy: She threw me out twice this week.
Mr. Malloy: It seems arbitrary. Outrageous.
Mrs. Malloy: Stupid rules. (*Truth*, 79–80)

This conversation shows ways in which these characters listen past each other. They focus on small details, such as whether the teacher is Mrs. or Miss. They allow their assumptions to constitute their listening rather than hearing out a speaker at greater length. When Philip finally tells his father that he merely wants to get out of the teacher's class, his father is already so swept up by the political ramifications—and potential for personal power—of this issue that Philip's truth gets lost.

At the same time, these parents clearly care about their child. Although it may simply be easier to believe Philip than to question him and to understand him, they come strongly to Philip's defense. They, like Philip, cannot accept his responsibility for a misunderstanding with Narwin; instead, they defend him so completely that they further distort the truth. Ted Griffen explodes Philip's small act of disobedience in his homeroom into a self-serving political issue in the name of personal rights, patriotism, the lack of morals taught in school, and, ultimately, the school budget. The larger the issue becomes and the more attention it receives, the more incomplete and misconstrued the truth becomes; the more public it becomes, the more it gets lost. Yet, the more unrecognizable the truth becomes, the more Philip begins to recognize the truth of his experience and his complicity in distorting it. By novel's end, the inability to communicate in a full, honest way results in Philip's tragic recognition of his loss and solidifies his isolation.

Even as the chronology and presentation of events force Philip and Narwin into opposition, Avi also compels readers to consider ways in which the situation makes the student and teacher alike. Early in the novel, Narwin applies for school funding to take a workshop in new methods of teaching English. While denying Narwin the money, Dr. Doane nevertheless compliments her on her success and value as a teacher. After removing Philip from her class for the second time, Narwin writes to her sister:

> So you see, Anita, it was gratifying to hear Gertrude [Doane]
> talk this way to me, exactly the kind of support teachers need.
> Certainly it's what I need at this time. I can't tell you how
> much. It bucks me up . . . I'm lucky. (*Truth*, 58)

Immediately following this letter, Avi includes an entry from
Philip's diary:

> Lots of kids bad-mouth their parents, say they never stick up for
> them or understand them. Or pay any attention to them. Stuff
> like that. My parents are different.
>   I'm lucky. (*Truth*, 58)

The back-to-back presentation of the letter and diary alerts readers to their shared sentiment and especially their shared language. Narwin and Philip consider themselves supported by
authority figures; both feel lucky.

Yet, these excerpts accelerate the novel's irony. Dr. Doane flat-
ters Narwin as she denies the teacher money for further education. Similarly, the earlier discussion demonstrates the misfortunes of miscommunication between Philip and his parents
rather than the fortuity expressed in this diary entry.

In fact, as the situation at school escalates, the polarization of
these two characters increases, and the misinformation generated
by their supporters (namely, Narwin's school administrators and
Philip's parents) becomes further distorted by the unwanted
assistance of outsiders. Once the media representatives enter the
picture, Narwin and Philip become more alike as they are pressed
continually into their adversarial positions. Similarly, as the story
expands beyond the realm of school and home and enters the
larger spheres reached by wire services, less factual information
is provided. Narwin and Philip lose distinction as individuals; various strains of the media typecast them in terms of what they
appear to represent; the situation ceases to be about a teacher-
student misunderstanding as it takes on the issues of censorship
and free expression. The resulting sensationalism smothers facts,
and, eventually, what happened between Narwin and Philip is of
no interest. The favorable letters that Philip receives suffocate

and isolate him because he knows that his actions carry no such nobility. Narwin receives only letters of reprimand, accusation, and castigation—none of which are based on knowledge of her or of the situation. Support of Narwin is quickly silenced, or—like Robert Duval, who wants to rewrite the original newspaper report about the event from Narwin's perspective—never voiced at all. As Narwin and Philip trust those with whom they feel lucky, they not only lose control over any possible interpersonal resolution but also become victims—not of each other but of an entire culture of misinformation and miscommunication.

At the point of their greatest polarization, Avi tenders Narwin and Philip as most alike. This time, Narwin speaks, rather than writes, to her sister, whereas Philip speaks to, rather than writes about, his father.

6:45 P.M.
Phone Conversation
between Margaret Narwin and Her Sister,
Anita Wigham

Anita Wigham: Peg, I am shocked!
Miss Narwin: Well, you can imagine how I felt. The dishonesty of it! And from Gertrude of all people. I still find it impossible to believe.
Anita Wigham: But what are you going to do?
Miss Narwin: Anita, I don't know. I truly don't know.

6:50 P.M.
Conversation
between Philip Malloy and His Father

Mr. Malloy: Philip, I want you to open the door so we can talk.
Philip Malloy: I don't want to talk.
Mr. Malloy: What happened in school?
Philip Malloy: Nothing. (*Truth*, 164–65)

Both characters admit, perhaps even recognize, their own powerlessness. As these two conversations clearly demonstrate, the security and the confidence they had in others as well as their own self-confidence have eroded. Subsequent events echo their abdication of all self-direction as Narwin and Philip retreat further and further. They pull into themselves and away from any opportunities for miscommunication as they reject communication altogether.

The novel moves from mostly written communication into primarily spoken exchanges. Narwin, the English teacher who advocates, practices, and explores the potency of words ironically no longer writes; almost as ironic is Philip's ignorance of the words of the national anthem. Not only does the written word appear more permanent than does the spoken, but it also proves more untrustworthy. Written communication burdens the word with the demand that it relate tone and attitude; it lacks the speaker's body language and intonation as partial bearers of message; in some ways, it must work harder to combine form and content. However, that does not mean that Avi suggests that the written word is more reliable than the spoken. Because of human nature, all forms of communication risk misunderstanding: Speakers and audiences each use their own codes, their own content and context. But messages can go astray, speakers and listeners may talk at cross-purposes, and content may contradict context. Although *Nothing but the Truth* "encourages readers to go beyond their natural self-absorption to posit the existence of other perspectives" (Rovenger, 21), it does not negotiate those variant perspectives for the reader. In fact, readers must remember that the novel, too, stands as simply one form of communication. To identify, to extract a truth from it may well be to misunderstand it. Avi's invisible narration fictionalizes his caution to the reader to "never fully trust the author, never fully trust my characters, never fully trust my story, no, not even my words" ("Seeing," 3). Words are untrustworthy, imperfect vehicles of communication. The readers may follow the author's direction, but they must generate their own meaning, their own elusive, even illusive, truth. It is no wonder that a book that trusts its young adult audience to resolve in individual ways such intricate, even enigmatic, issues not only earned recognition as a Newbery Honor Book but also continues to secure a substantial readership.

6. Avi as Truthteller

You don't know about me, without you have read a book by the
name of "The Adventures of Tom Sawyer," but that ain't no
matter. That book was made by Mr. Mark Twain, and he told
the truth, mainly. There was things which he stretched, but
mainly he told the truth. That is nothing. I never seen anybody
but lied, one time or another, without it was Aunt Polly, or the
widow, or maybe Mary. Aunt Polly—Tom's Aunt Polly she is—
and Mary, and the Widow Douglas, is all told about in that
book—which is mostly a true book; with some stretchers, as I
said before.

—Mark Twain, *The Adventures of Huckleberry Finn*[1]

Ursula K. LeGuin writes that the "young creature does need protection and shelter. But it also needs the truth. And it seems to
me that the way you can speak absolutely honestly and factually
to a child about both good and evil is to talk about himself. Himself, his inner self, his deep, the deepest Self. That is something
he can cope with; indeed, his job in growing up is to become himself."[2] In *Sometimes I Think I Hear My Name, Devil's Race,* and
The True Confessions of Charlotte Doyle, Avi positions adolescent
characters between the protection and shelter created by adults
and the dislodgings established when lies break into truths.
These three novels treat ways in which hearing and telling the
truth impel the adolescent toward adulthood. LeGuin refers to
Jung's archetypal shadow in discussing the child's necessary
recognition and ultimate incorporation of the difficult, darker
aspects of self in order to be whole. These three novels trace the
steps of that path toward completeness: In searching for his par-

ents, Conrad learns truths about them that are dissonant with his expectations; John Proud confronts his shadow-side; and Charlotte Doyle tells her story from an understanding of self as changing and mutable, a self whose shadow has been recognized, confronted, and incorporated, a self that has learned the elusive nature of truth.

Sometimes I Think I Hear My Name

Conrad Murray, the 13-year-old protagonist in *Sometimes I Think I Hear My Name*, feels suffocated by the protection and shelter offered by his Aunt Lu and Uncle Carl in their St. Louis home. His aunt and uncle, Conrad's surrogate parents since he was nine years old, provide the constancy and emotional stability Conrad's parents felt they could not provide after their divorce. Conrad's parents live apart in New York City, each pursuing their individual dreams although leaving Conrad behind.

This first-person novel opens with Conrad's perception that he protects and takes care of his aunt and uncle by "not saying what was on [his] mind."[3] This pretense becomes the key to Conrad's personality. He seldom says what is on his mind; instead, he lives a dual life of masquerade in which appearances and reality eventually conflict. Conrad lies to others about his parents, partly to prove himself worthy to his friends, partly out of shame at his parents' abandonment of him, and partly in order to deny his own disappointment at not really knowing his parents. Rather than accepting the semester-break trip to England given to him by his aunt and uncle, Conrad lies to his caretakers and reorganizes his trip to go to New York City and to visit his long-absent parents.

Aunt Lu and Uncle Carl feed Conrad's disillusionment about his mother and father. Although meaning well, Lu and Carl portray Conrad's parents as wholly loving people who "wanted most of all for you to have a stable, happy home" (*Name*, 7). Lu and Carl describe parents who care about and want Conrad as part of their lives. When Conrad participates in their self-deceptive portrayal, Lu and Carl deflect his misunderstandings and avoid any genuine, honest conversation about Conrad's parents. Under the guise of protection and shelter, they withhold the powerful truth about Conrad's selfish, childish mother and father.

Conrad crafts an elaborate lie to wangle his way to New York. Encountering Nancy Sperling in a travel agency, he overhears her plans to travel home to the city during the semester break at her private school. In order to see Nancy, Conrad dresses up and masquerades to school officials as her brother. Conrad proposes to Nancy that they exchange places: She will fly to England on his tickets, and he will venture to New York on hers. Despite sensing that Nancy is ill at ease, that something is wrong with her, Conrad initially reveals to her the truth about his visit and his desire to switch tickets. However, "the truth wasn't working. [He] switched back to a story" (*Name*, 21). This story continues the extensive lies about his parents, about his aunt and uncle, and about himself.

Nancy counters Conrad's storytelling with a truthtelling that Conrad interprets as fabulous lies. Avi's ironic juxtaposition of lies and truth in this exchange reveals the relative normalcy of Conrad's nuclear family with Aunt Lu and Uncle Carl as it calls into question the stability of Nancy's family, where the parents live one apartment up from their children.

Avi arranges the book chronologically as a way to impose order on the chaos created by Conrad's lies and on the confusion Conrad suffers in learning the truth about his parents. The chapters are broken into days, and the days of Conrad's spring vacation spent illicitly in New York are divided into portions of days. Conrad's report follows the regular movement of the calendar until so much disturbance fills one day that it must be rendered in parts. The novel's structure offers a metaphoric understanding of Conrad himself: He tells his story in order, although it reveals one seeking order—yet not in control of it; he proposes a wholeness to his story—and to himself—when, in fact, both he and his story are composed of fragments that constantly shift into new patterns of knowledge. Whereas his story follows a regular order, his life proves as kaleidoscopic, as metamorphic as Nancy's butterfly tattoo.

Of course, Conrad's life seems relatively organized when compared to the disarray he finds at Nancy's New York apartment,
where he arrives without having informed his parents or his aunt
and uncle. Even though he had initially told Nancy the truth
about wanting to be in New York, Conrad finds that at Nancy's
apartment others admit to lying but his lying is challenged. Her
sister demands to know his true name and identity.

> "Look, Murray, or Buckingham, or Conrad, or whatever your
> name is," said the sister, lighting a cigarette, "you seem like an
> okay kid. But we don't believe you. What's the real story? What
> do you want from Nancy?"
> I was so surprised by that, I couldn't answer. I turned to
> Nancy to see if I could get any help from her. She gave me noth-
> ing. I was beginning to wonder if she even knew how to smile.
> "I mean," continued the sister, "you act as if you've been kid-
> napped or something. That's a lot of crap. Then you told me that
> your name was Murray, but you told Nancy, here, it was Buck-
> ingham. Which is it?"
> "Conrad Murray," I said.
> I looked at Nancy again, trying to convince myself that she
> was looking at me in a nice way, but I couldn't be sure if that
> was true. Sometimes I thought it was, but mostly there was
> nothing on her face at all.
> "Look," said the sister, "we're not going to *do* anything to
> you for not telling the truth. I happen to lie a lot myself. Big
> deal. But you're coming to us for help, right? So we have to
> know. *What is happening?*"
> "I never said I was kidnapped," I said. Too upset to make up
> anything else, I decided to try the truth. (*Name*, 46–47)

Conrad begins to share with Nancy and her sister his family's circumstances and the reasons for his visit to New York. With the
perspicacity of someone negotiating her own family relationships,
Nancy's sister immediately points to the possibility—the fact
even—that his parents do not want to see him. Despite his denial,
her revelation made him "feel ashamed, even dirty" (*Name*, 48).
The squalor of the girls' apartment exposes the shame they feel
about their rejection by their parents. By cleaning their apartment, Conrad not only repays them for letting him stay with

them, but, more importantly, it symbolizes his slow awakening to and acceptance of his parents' rejection.

In this work of realistic fiction, Conrad sees his world through the lens of hyperbole. He originally considers Nancy a zombie and her sister Pat, a vampire. Perceiving his parents in equally extreme ways, he believes they truly love him even though they seldom contact him and never see him. According to Conrad, his father Noel does not simply work for Macy's department store—he runs it. Conrad's visit indeed surprises his father, catching him at an inopportune time. The visit hints at the many ways in which Conrad has romanticized this father-son relationship—and the ways in which Noel cannot meet even the basic demands of parenting. The father can imagine only one reason for his son's sudden appearance: Conrad is in some kind of trouble that requires Noel's help. The idea that Conrad wants to see him and get to know him remains incomprehensible to Noel. Not knowing Conrad as a son, or at all, Noel attempts to treat Conrad as a friend, offering to double-date with him and to meet Conrad for lunch. Conrad leaves the interaction unsettled, not knowing "what to say, to feel, to think" (*Name*, 90). Conrad's inflated view of his perfect father flattens against the disappointing sharpness of the reality of Noel.

Conrad persists in pursuing his mother. Tracking her down, he sees a one-woman band, an unbelievable circus image:

> [I] could not believe what I saw. It was my mother, all dressed up in a costume, an Uncle Sam costume, with red-and-white striped pants, a string tie, and a high hat studded with stars. Hanging from her chin was this phony-looking, scraggly goat beard.
>
> She was sitting beside, or behind, or in this thing: a bass drum with bells hanging on it, as well as balloons of all colors, and three squeeze horns, too. In one hand she held a big drumstick that was streaming with ribbons. In the other hand she had a silver trumpet. On her arms were jingle bells. (*Name*, 109)

This reintroduction to his mother presents Conrad with both masquerade and truth. Quite literally, she wears a costume; however, this "luckless childlike"[4] actor makes a career out of pretense. Unfortunately for Conrad, she lacks adequate acting ability to convince in her role as parent. This encounter, like that with his father, sickens Conrad and jolts him into realizing that "Aunt Lu and Uncle Carl were probably right not to want me to [come]. I guess they were protecting me" (*Name*, 117).

One more interaction with irregular parents awaits Conrad. Nancy invites Conrad to dinner at her parents' upstairs apartment. In this scene especially, "Avi offers an almost surrealistic view of family life" (Cooper, 1308). Conrad finds their apartment sterile, the order stressed and stressful in contrast to the chaos of the apartment he has shared with Nancy and Pat. He marks the oddity of Nancy's dressing up in her girlish school uniform for dinner. Throughout the strained silence of dinner, the unsuccessful pretense of the Sperlings as good parents dawns on Conrad. Partially spurred by Aunt Lu's anger at his mother, Conrad finally breaks through the quiescence with an eruption of truthtelling about himself and his family. Despite polite requests to stop, Conrad continues to spew forth his newfound knowledge about his parents and makes an oath to always tell the truth. The Sperlings' masquerade as parents and as a family causes Conrad's epiphany.

Conrad comes to terms with being a divorced child, and Nancy shares with him how she survives her parents' divorce from her. She confesses to Conrad the guilt she feels about causing her parents' unhappiness, about her desire to free them of herself—and to free herself of them.

> "I thought of running away. Of killing myself. But I was too frightened to do those things.
>
> "One day I was walking in the park. A butterfly went by. I reached out, tried to catch it. It only darted away. I ran after it, but always it flew out of reach. And when I gave up at last, the butterfly flew away, free, impossible to catch. But it gave me my idea. . . .
>
> "Then I said to myself, the butterfly is me. I kill the rest. I won't see, or feel, or say anything. No one will be able to touch what is really me." (*Name*, 133–34)

In explaining to Conrad the sustaining power of her butterfly tattoo, Nancy acknowledges her family's deceit and reveals her own masquerade. She exposes the butterfly as symbolic and opens up the living parts of herself to Conrad. Before they part, the two hold each other in a sleep of innocent, vulnerable touching. The novel's conclusion shows Conrad returning to the nurturing parentage of Aunt Lu and Uncle Carl and working to sustain, even to develop, a friendship with Nancy. Thus Conrad begins to build a life and relationships based on truth.

In discussing the genesis of this novel, Avi writes that it "is based on a) the particular living circumstances of a kid I knew; b) a remark about locale by a writer friend; c) a passing reference by my wife to the way some kids were living; d) the off-chance remark of another friend about a parent; and e) a quote from Ross MacDonald, 'Most fiction is shaped by geography and permeated by autobiography, even when it is not trying to be.' "[5] These five elements converge in a novel about the difficult ground of developing self-identity. Like kids, particular and universal, Conrad travels away from home only to discover himself, only to learn how much of himself resides at home. Avi parallels Conrad's aimless rides through the streets of New York with Conrad's journey toward self-truths. Still a child, although one who knows himself better, Conrad returns to St. Louis, to the protection and shelter of home.

Devil's Race

John Proud, the 16-year-old protagonist in *Devil's Race*, leaves the security of home and school to explore the historical terrain of family. In search of what he "needed to know about [his] family,"[6] John meets unexamined, darker sides of himself. "This story of John and his namesake ancestor provides a suspenseful ghost story with supernatural overtones, and hints of the good and evil within us all. . . ."[7] The confident, popular, and proud John learns not only that he casts a shadow but also that his "shadow stands on the threshold" ("Shadow," 54) of self-knowledge; his task, then, is to meet that shadow and recognize it in himself and himself in it.

Avi breaks *Devil's Race* into four parts. These segments, all related in a first-person narration, monitor John Proud's movement into a divided self, the potential domination by his shadow-self, a confrontation with his shadow-self, and ultimately the incorporation of his darker side into a more complete self-identity.

In his quest to learn more about his family history, John invokes the help of his Uncle David, who discloses that John's "great-great-great-great-grandfather, John Proud, was hanged in the year 1854. . . . He was a demon" (*Race*, 7). After reading the obituary, John's curiosity becomes fueled by his uneasiness at being named after what the newspaper article describes as "this grim visage of evil" (*Race*, 8). Together, John and Uncle Dave travel to Lickdale, Pennsylvania, for a weekend visit to the gravesite of the first John Proud.

John and Uncle Dave plan to spend the weekend with the family of a distant cousin, Nora Fenton, who lives ten miles from the cemetery. Although welcoming in every way, Nora reacts negatively to the proposed graveyard investigation. Her outburst of explanation about the activities and nature of the first John Proud initiate the division of John's self.

> "Fun!" cried Nora. She turned to me. "Your namesake liked to hurt people. He would win their trust, then betray them. Torment them, destroy them. Murder them, in fact. No one could have been crueler. He used people in the worst possible way."
> All of a sudden I felt anger toward her. It came out of nowhere.
> That anger, quick as it came, caught me by surprise. I tried to push it away. (*Race*, 17–18)

Ann, Nora's daughter, also tries to warn John. Her general ease and comfort with people echo John's self-confidence, and her athleticism and her knowledge of the Wilderness reservation appeal to him. Although they genuinely like each other, she does not dissuade John from exploring the cemetery simply by declaring that "once was enough." When neither her mother nor her father can trailblaze for John and Uncle Dave, Nora reluctantly consents to act as guide.

Threading their way through the woods toward the cemetery, Uncle Dave initially pushes ahead "as if he were giving a challenge, or a warning" (*Race*, 30). Yet, the closer they get, the farther back David falls until, finally, he declares that he is ill. Nearly there, David attends to his failing physical condition and takes it as a sign not to proceed. He demands that John not follow through, that they all turn back—"it's a mistake" (*Race*, 39). However, John Proud has earned his allegorical name, and his prideful ego forces him on to find the site and to render complete his self-division: "My heart turned over. My own grave. My name. Standing there I felt split in two" (*Race*, 42).

That feeling quickly turns to disappointment, which leads to a stream of accusations against Uncle Dave and Ann for building up false excitement. As they leave the gravesite, John's warm feelings for the others return so that when David needs water, John runs back to the grave to retrieve the canteen. The return raises the ghost of the past John Proud into the shadow image of the current John Proud.

> [S]itting atop the stone was a boy, a teenager, fairly tall, somewhat on the thin side. He looked like anybody and nobody, a perfectly normal-looking kid. But he was oddly familiar, like someone I had met once, yet could not quite recall. . . .
> With a shock I realized why he looked so familiar. I was staring at a mirror image.
> *He was me.* (*Race*, 44)

At this point the novel becomes increasingly complicated. In Ursula K. LeGuin's understanding of the child and his or her shadow, John Proud, like Ged in *A Wizard of Earthsea*, first raises his shadow, then recognizes it, and ultimately must name it, claim it, and incorporate it. Like Ged, the archmage of Earthsea, Avi's young John Proud rejects the shadow he has raised. The past John Proud confides to his namesake that he knows that "somewhere in you, John, is something very different . . ." (*Race*, 48). The difference can be seen only by the evil of the past John

Proud because it is the potential for evil in young John. Young John counters this accusation with a defense, a rejection: " 'That's not true,' I insisted, 'it's not!' " (*Race*, 49).

This rejection empowers the past John Proud to haunt the present. Identities overlap as the young John Proud watches his negative thoughts turn into realized actions. When Uncle Dave is hospitalized from the stress of the incident and then dies, John believes that "[i]t was as if my *thinking* had made it happen. Hadn't I wanted him out of the way? Hadn't I wished him to disappear?" (*Race*, 64) The events and John's feelings of complicity in causing them escalate throughout this chapter. Others begin to see John, although he knows it is the ghost of John Proud they see. As he questions these hauntings, he believes the ghost causes them; however, this demonstrates John's fearful projection of his evil impulses onto the ghost of John Proud. Rather than recognize and claim these darker desires, the young John Proud disowns them and puts them onto another.

As the tension between the two John Prouds builds, the younger finds himself increasingly interested in pursuing a relationship with Ann. Yet, his consuming attention to his divided self distracts him and pushes her away; they grow apart even as they try to draw together. As they work to communicate with each other, Ann suggests to young John that he needs to return to the gravesite. Even though frightened and unsure, he concedes: "I knew more than ever that what she had said was right. I had to get out there and face John Proud. I had to know who was doing all these things. Was it him . . . or me?" (*Race*, 80) Although John approaches a confrontation with the darker side of himself, he still indulges the division of self.

Ann accompanies John on his return journey to John Proud's 1854 grave. As they prepare for their mission, young John begins to entertain the possibility that he is connected in some way to the ghost. He confides to Ann his greatest fear:

> "Look, Ann, if he's my opposite, and I'm trying to get rid of him
> . . . well, see, this is one of those big questions: Doesn't it figure

he's trying to do the same thing to me, you know, get rid of me?"
(*Race*, 85)

Once he articulates this potential connection, the urgency of the
journey increases. It swells again when the ghost reaches out to
John and when it also threatens Ann. This move challenges the
young John not only to claim the shadowed aspects of himself but
also, and perhaps more importantly, to save the positive side, the
goodness, love, and trust that Ann awakens in him.

The return to the graveyard, then, becomes a confrontation
with evil and an acceptance of goodness for the young John
Proud. On the journey into the Wilderness, John continues to
indulge his dividedness; unable to admit that he raised the ghost,
he asks self-absorbed questions like "why me?"—questions that
only cast suspicion on others and continue to block self-knowledge. In a moment of insight, John realizes he cannot return to
the burial ground because he possesses no power there, whereas
the ghost is all-powerful at the grave. John chooses Devil's Race
as the site of his confrontation.

The ghost visits John during Ann's trip to get water. This
exchange proves essential because the ghost is able to manipulate
John's own fear and self-doubt to turn Ann against him. The
ghost/shadow is about to consume John and his goodness. However, as John suspects Ann, he starts to wish her away and to
accuse her of betraying him. His dismissal of her keeps her safely
away from the scene of his final encounter. LeGuin would contend that the showdown between the shadow and the self cannot
be witnessed; it must be fought on the individual ground of selfhood.

John truly begins to pursue the ghost when he realizes that he
was responsible and that he "did not want [Ann] to know that
truth—that evil—in [him]" (*Race*, 141). Now the active chaser, he
harnesses his capacity to hate as the weapon with which to
destroy the ghost of John Proud. However, because he raised the
ghost, it functions, too, as his shadow and John knows definitively that

If I destroyed him, that very act would make me him. *That* was
what he wanted. My hatred would match his. And he would
then be able to take my place. That would be his ultimate victory, his triumph. (*Race*, 148)

John faces his shadow and claims it.

> They were not separate. They were one. As we were. Insepa-
> rable.
> And I knew then the only way to save myself.
> Instantly, I leaped upon him. But instead of trying to kill
> him, I embraced him. . . . All I knew was that I must not let him
> go. I must hold him, accept him.
> In the middle of that field of fire, locked together, he now in
> terror, as I was, we were equal—good, bad—two parts of one
> come together at last. (*Race*, 149)

Ann's pennywhistle call signals her forgiveness, her goodness and
his, and leads John back.

Devil's Race indeed proves to be a "psychological thriller"[8] that
dramatizes an adolescent's psychic journey toward the wholeness
of self-knowledge. Unlike Conrad, who must turn his lies around
to locate their truths, young John Proud must assemble the
pieces of truth into a composite whole. Both Conrad and John
return home at their stories' end; however, Conrad's home is one
in which others offer sheltered protection in which he can grow,
whereas John's home is the residence of his wholly formed self.

The True Confessions of Charlotte Doyle

The True Confessions of Charlotte Doyle posits yet a more sophisticated understanding of the adolescent's journey toward the
home of self. Because Charlotte immediately labels her story a
confession, her journey has been completed before its telling
begins. Her confrontation and incorporation of her shadow-side
into a complete and resilient self informs her narration at every
point. Even though John Proud narrates *Devil's Race* in the past
tense, the tale reads as if the events occurred in the present. Con-

versely, a self-conscious perspective on the past characterizes Charlotte's voice. "That growth of *self*-awareness energies the book."[9] Although John Proud and Conrad tell their stories as if they did not know their endings, Charlotte's final episode enlivens, even directs, her telling.

John's and Conrad's stories belong to memory; Charlotte's belongs to rememory because it tenders "an exquisitely textured recollection, real or imagined, which is otherwise indescribable."[10] *The True Confessions of Charlotte Doyle* realizes texture on three distinct levels. First, Avi imagines the story of Charlotte Doyle and crafts the novel to tell it. On the next level, Avi's character, Charlotte, keeps a journal in which she records "in perfect detail everything that transpired during that fateful voyage across the Atlantic Ocean in the summer of 1832."[11] Yet, when Charlotte's father burns that journal for its "unfortunate capacity to invent the most outlandish, not to say *unnatural* tales" (*Charlotte*, 207), Charlotte reconstructs the journal and "set[s] down secretly what had happened during the voyage . . . [as] a way of fixing all the details . . . forever" (*Charlotte*, 208).

The novel, then, stands as a dual act of historiography. In choosing a historical setting, Avi imagines history, an act of rewriting history through contemporary eyes. And Charlotte composes her own history as she recreates from memory the burned journal describing her voyage.

Avi textures this narrative with a commanding use of language as one way of setting the novel historically. Charlotte attends the Barrington School for Better Girls (*Charlotte*, 2), where she learns the proper comportment for the daughters of wealthy families. When Charlotte gets her first look at the crew of the *Seahawk*, on which she is about to cross the Atlantic Ocean, her thoughts convey a language and an attitude that place her in the early nineteenth century. She thinks:

> I mounted the steps to the quarterdeck. When I reached the top the captain was moving away from me. Grateful for the momentary reprieve, I stood where I was, fighting the nausea I felt, gathering all my womanly arts so as to present myself in the

102 PRESENTING AVI

most agreeable fashion, making sure my hair, my best asset, fell
just so—despite the breeze—to my lower back. (*Charlotte*, 30)

References to now-historical children's novels—*Story of a Bad
Boy* and *What Katy Did*—further establish the time of the book as
does Charlotte's appearance "as a young woman, bonnet covering
[her] beautiful hair, full skirts, high button shoes, and, you may
be sure, white gloves" (*Charlotte*, 1). The active loading dock
clearly belongs to the nineteenth century: They pack not only
"bales of silk and tobacco! Chests of tea!" (*Charlotte*, 8) but also
parrots and monkeys. Although Charlotte finds the scene somewhat chaotic, the large number of ships loading for departure and
the items they carry depict a seafaring economy.

The names Avi uses combine historical detail with literary references. Names such as Grummage—and especially Jaggery—
mimic the Dickensian tradition of using names and their sounds
to hint at character—even Doyle suggests Charlotte's original
primness. Effective similes fix visual images that often further
characterizations. Avi introduces Zachariah as looking "like the
very imp of death in search of souls . . . His arms and legs were as
thin as marlin spikes. His face, as wrinkled as a crumpled napkin
. . ." (*Charlotte*, 20); indeed, Zachariah does conspire with death
in order to save Charlotte's soul.

To structure the novel, Avi borrows from Victorian melodramas. "A rousing adventure story set in times past, this tale fea-
turing a female protagonist has all the suspense, derring-do, and
pacing of Stevenson's *Kidnapped*."[12] The novel has both a prologue, Charlotte's "Important Warning," and an appendix, not a
full epilogue, but a postconclusion installation of information useful in understanding the novel. The prologue hooks the audience
immediately, but it is Avi's end-of-chapter cliff-hangers that bait
readers. Chapter 8 ends with Charlotte's stating "[B]ut the storm
was—at first—man-made" (*Charlotte*, 70). At times, these cliff-
hangers achieve a disconcerting symmetry. Chapter 17 concludes
with Captain Jaggery telling Charlotte that her "trial com-
mences" (*Charlotte*, 158), whereas the next chapter ends with
Charlotte's resigned declaration that "[t]he trial was over" (*Char-*

lotte, 170). These are the endings of a master storyteller who commands plot and story while foreshadowing events and changes in character.

Charlotte's reconstruction of her original journal slowly reveals her transformation. Her awareness of its outcome enables her to structure the telling, to translate the passage of chaotic events into a fictional, understandable whole, to anticipate and foretell. This second journal, more fictional than the first one, which her father condemns as "rubbish of the worst taste. Stuff for penny dreadfuls!" (*Charlotte*, 207), benefits from the perspective Charlotte has gained.

Charlotte's rewriting of her own recent history begins with a recognition of her former self, whose destiny was to be a lady (*Charlotte*, 1). The early Charlotte stands as a product of her economic and social class. Although class imposed limits based on gender, Charlotte benefited from belonging to a wealthy family. She carries on board a trunk of great weight and size, a trunk neatly packed by her school maids. Charlotte is initially concerned with escorts, with reading material to fill the hours of boredom, and with appearance. She considers the crew "as sorry a group of men as I had ever seen: glum in expression, defeated in posture, with no character in any eye save sullenness. They were like men recruited from the doormat of Hell" (*Charlotte*, 26). Her sense of propriety and of her entitlement as a member of the upper class demand that she set herself apart from the crew, even that she treat them as servants whose purpose is to add to her personal comfort.

Like her privileged parents, Charlotte judges others by their appearance. When she meets Captain Jaggery, she judges him as a social equal.

> From his fine coat, from his tall beaver hat, from his glossy black boots, from his clean, chiseled countenance, from the dignified way he carried himself, I knew at once—without having to be told—that this must be Captain Jaggery. And he—I saw in a glance—was a gentleman, the kind of man I was used to. A man to be trusted. In short, a man to whom I could talk and upon whom I could rely. (*Charlotte*, 27)

Charlotte allies herself with someone whose precise, ordered appearance appeals to her. Fatefully, she moves from appraising the captain as a social peer to valuing him as a moral equal. In Captain Jaggery, Charlotte recognizes the clothing and comportment of her father. Her quick projection of her father onto Captain Jaggery makes complete sense: About to embark as the only female and the only child on an extended journey, Charlotte seeks the adult protection and guidance she has always known. Charlotte again casts Captain Jaggery as her father: She "tried the garments [made by Zachariah for her] on, finding them surprisingly comfortable until, shocked, [she] remembered [her]self. Hurriedly, [she] took them off, resolving not to stoop so low again" (*Charlotte*, 66–67). Then she goes to have tea with the captain and reads to him her self-assigned essay on "the proper behavior for young women" (*Charlotte*, 67). The novel's ending proves that the similarities between the captain and Charlotte's father reach well below surface appearances.

True and false appearances seesaw throughout the novel as deceptions increase. Characters masquerade for a variety of reasons. Second mate Keetch professes loyalty to the crew while in league with the captain to put himself in a better position. The crew stages a funeral for Zachariah to ensure that knowledge about the captain reaches port authorities. Charlotte's desperate desire for protection and for constancy in her old world make possible Captain Jaggery's pretense as father figure. Yet, when she sees Jaggery first shoot Cranick cold-bloodedly and then choose Zachariah to bear the punishment for the mutiny, Charlotte no longer believes that his appearance exhibits the true man. Conversely, whereas Charlotte originally rejects Zachariah's gift of sailor's clothing, the end of part 1 depicts Charlotte shedding her old attire and donning the new clothes. Her final statement that she had become "one of the crew" (*Charlotte*, 106) stresses that the new garments transcend mere costume to act as definers of Charlotte's changing identity. Perhaps the most important instance of masquerade carries the greatest irony. Charlotte originally considers the crew as a disreputable lot and shows only modest hesitation in revealing their mutinous plot. Jaggery says that "it took only this girl . . . to unmask" (*Charlotte*, 88) them. In fact, Jaggery's retribution for the mutiny exposes his true nature while Charlotte genuinely unmasks the crew as she becomes one of them. Up until this point in her narrative, the sailors have remained a faceless backdrop to Charlotte's polite social exchanges with the agreeable captain. Now, they become individuals whose faces and names she knows. The final masquerade belongs to Charlotte. Now a fully complexioned sailor, Charlotte changes back into her proper young lady's clothing to meet her family when the ship docks.

> I went to my cabin and excitedly dressed myself in the clothes I had kept for the occasion: bonnet over my mangled hair. Full if somewhat ragged skirts. Shoes rather less than intact. Gloves more gray than white. To my surprise I felt so much pinched and confined I found it difficult to breathe. I glanced at my trunk where I had secreted my sailor's garb as a tattered memento. For a moment I considered changing back to that, but quickly reminded myself that it must—from then on—remain a memento. (*Charlotte*, 198–99)

Charlotte soon learns that life with her family, in their impeccably ordered and maintained home, would require her always to put on a facade. Her final decision to change again into sailor's garb marks the truth of her confessions and of the identity she discovers aboard ship.

As she leaves her protective boarding school to travel on the *Seahawk,* Charlotte moves from one form of confinement to another. Avi asserts that this story stems from a reader's comment about *Something Upstairs* as a locked-room story, and "it occurred to [him] that a tale of murder on a ship at sea might be considered a 'locked room' mystery."[13] Indeed, the ship at sea physically replicates a locked room from which escape is ruled out. By extension, the locked room serves as an apt metaphor to describe the psychological realities endured by those at sea—and by Charlotte especially. The ship imprisons one in that it sets forth a definitive hierarchy of responsibility and prescribes adherence to a chain of command. Charlotte experiences a claustrophobia on board ship that readers understand to exemplify the repression imposed by Charlotte's class and, particularly, by her father. When first shown her quarters, she reflects:

> during my life I had never once—not for a moment—been without the support, the guidance, the *protection* of my elders, you will accept my words as being without exaggeration when I tell you that at that moment I was certain I had been placed in a coffin. *My* coffin. (*Charlotte*, 20)

In addition to anticipating the pall of death that will influence the novel's plot, this passage correlates the adult protection characterizing her early life to a coffinlike restraint. Her descriptions of the ship belowdecks, in which Charlotte expects—and is expected—to stay focus on the small size of everything, from her cabin, which cannot contain her trunk, to the galley stool and passageways. Her space, like her freedoms, is limited.

Avi employs images of dark and light to underscore effectively this literal and metaphorical oppressiveness. As Zachariah leads Charlotte to her cabin, "[h]ere and there lanterns glowed; masts, spars, and rigging vaguely sketched the dim outlines of the net in which [she] felt caught" (*Charlotte*, 21). With the assistance and friendship of this old black man, who sees his commonality with Charlotte's status as outsider among the ship's crew, Charlotte begins to detect the contours of her restrained life. Not only does Zachariah extend the hand of friendship, but also he offers her a risky protection: Unlike the adults in her parents' world, Zachariah cannot guard her innocence from what he knows will be a mutinous trip; however, in giving her the dirk, he insists upon her self-protection. Zachariah moves Charlotte outside the dark circle of childish naïveté and egotism and into the illuminated circle of adult awareness and responsibility.

Charlotte resists Zachariah and the knowledge with which he wishes to equip her. Instead, she reaches out to Jaggery, a reminder of her father and, by extension, of the safety of her old world. Curiously, however, Jaggery, like Zachariah, threatens Charlotte's retreat into the world of comfort when he tells her of the round-robin as a sign of mutiny and describes the danger to all on board should he lose control. Charlotte responds to this powerful information not by grasping Zachariah's dagger as a means of self-protection but instead by offering it to the captain, thus negating her ability to protect herself and seeking his protection of her. The captain refuses that responsibility when he insists, as does Zachariah, that Charlotte keep the knife, that she accept responsibility for herself.

Images of light and dark weave throughout Charlotte's journey toward Providence, Rhode Island—and her journey toward herself. Although she expects a dazzling sky, one of "menacing clay-like gray" (*Charlotte*, 33) greets her. On the trip, Charlotte learns the crew's desire for revenge against the captain, and her sense of an ominous voyage escalates. At this point in the novel, it remains dramatically unclear about who the reader—and Charlotte—should align with images of dark and those of light. Is the darkness here because the crew is plotting mutiny, because they cannot be trusted and intend to betray? Charlotte's next venture clarifies some of the alliances. The captain escorts her above board, and she "felt like a princess being led to her throne" (*Charlotte*, 49). Even though the day remains dismal, "a thin yellow disk began to appear where [the captain] pointed, though it soon faded again behind clotted clouds" (*Charlotte*, 49). Charlotte casts Captain Jaggery as the source of light; however, the chapter continues to offer provocative illumination that complicates Charlotte's drive to identify the captain as the source of good. She learns that the captain sails with a brig—a jail on board ship—and gets a glimmer of the ship's stowaway. In short, the truth about captain and crew begins to fracture Charlotte's heretofore simple separation of the world into light and dark, good and evil based on visible appearance.

Near the novel's end, Charlotte returns to the captain's quarters—this time not to visit but to steal from him the key to his gun case in order to advance the crew's insurrection. Charlotte sees again the captain's quarters, not in the flattering concealment of the moon, but in the light. "Take away the light and . . . Everything appears in order" (*Charlotte*, 190). She is quick to recognize the captain's madness mimicked in the cabin's disrepair.

Similarly, images of light increasingly describe Zachariah and the crew. These quiet glows persist, much as Zachariah's faithfulness to her perseveres despite her doubts, as the light sharpens her understanding of the complex gloom. The "dim outlines" that Charlotte initially thinks will entrap her flesh out into full silhouettes to become the shadows of Captain Jaggery and her father, figures that threaten her identity, her life.

More than anything else, *The True Confessions of Charlotte Doyle* speaks less about a 13-year-old girl's transformation and more to her discovery of herself as she forms a solid, personal identity. Charlotte's trial for the murder of first mate Hollybrass tests the integrity of her newfound identity as a member of the crew and reveals the varied complexion of morality in an arena in which truth sees easy, even necessary, distortion. When the captain puts Charlotte on trial for the murder, both Charlotte and the crew remain unsure about the true perpetrator; therefore, Charlotte can mount only a partial defense. She and the crew refuse to reveal Zachariah, whom they assume Jaggery thinks is dead, and to betray Zachariah, who had motive and opportunity to commit the murder. Instead, she falls victim to the captain's methodical, shrewdly close-ended questions, to which a declarative "yes" or "no" misdirect truth. The captain extends to Charlotte the choice of her identity: trial as a crew member or immunity because she is the shipowner's privileged daughter. Charlotte's decision to maintain her fulfilling identity as crew member fuels the captain's successful prosecution of her as unnatural and therefore guilty. In revealing Charlotte's defiance of accepted, even expected, gender and social roles, Jaggery facilely allows the crew to betray Charlotte; although they may have accepted her as an equal, they deeply believe her guilty of acting unnaturally.

Once home in Providence, Charlotte's father also condemns her as unnatural. Here, however, she does not have a fair trial, and she suffers when "her beloved papa [acts] very much like the captain, tyrannical and unyielding."[14] Rather than interrogate Charlotte about the truth of her voyage, he silences her spoken voice while burning the journal to obliterate her written voice. These actions pose a choiceless choice of identity to Charlotte: Staying at home would require her to live in a house "immense . . . and dark. Cut off . . . from sun and air" (*Charlotte*, 201). She can no longer live as this abiding daughter because she no longer is that person. The voyage dislodges Charlotte from the shelter of adults, breaks some shackles of gender and class roles, and forces her to relocate her self, to claim her identity as independent sailor and rejoin the ship's crew.

The strength of this novel's voice, its characterization, its high-seas adventure story, and its historical detail won critical and popular acclaim. The novel received starred reviews in *School Library Journal, Booklist*, and *The Horn Book* and garnered a pointer in *Kirkus*. It also won the *Boston Globe-Horn Book* Award for Fiction and was named a Newbery Honor Book. While young readers continued to revel in his engaging stories, "innovative mixture[s] of history and fiction . . . [and] chilling realism,"[15] this list of impressive recognitions marked a heightened critical respect for Avi's work. In his acceptance for the *Boston Globe-Horn Book* award, Avi writes that he remains "enthralled with the idea and act of writing, the capture of ideas, the design of plot, the finding and shaping of words, the struggle to discover the real truths that lurk within the hearts of imagined souls."[16] In the "improbable but deeply satisfying conclusion" (Mercier, 57) to *The True Confessions of Charlotte Doyle*, Avi stays loyal to the truths discovered about Charlotte while the locked-room of the novel holds verities to be uncovered by readers.

In discussing his work, Avi often traces the development of one story or book into other books. Although he reports that *The True Confessions of Charlotte Doyle* had roots in *The Man Who Was Poe* (*Book Links*), other female characters created by Avi anticipate Charlotte Doyle. Like Elizabeth in *Encounter at Easton*, Charlotte opts to run away rather than live in a restrictive environment. In many ways, Emily Upham anticipates Charlotte Doyle. Both are rooted in Victoriana, both are shaped heavily by the Victorian culture with its social expectations and prescriptions. However, where Avi instills *Emily Upham's Revenge* with a comedic critical commentary that enables readers to laugh at some of Emily's more ridiculous mannerisms, he endows Charlotte with the complexity and awareness to realize society's restrictions—and to break free from them. One might consider Charlotte Doyle to be Emily Upham, grown up complete with an integrated shadow-self. Like Cathleen in *Captain Grey*, Charlotte commands her intelligence, her wit, and her insight; Charlotte moves beyond Cathleen as her seafaring adventure mirrors her growth as an independent and flexible thinker. Like *Bright Shadow*'s Morwenna, Charlotte and all of these characters present females, girls-growing-into-women, as strong and individual; to some extent all are feminist. However, with Charlotte Doyle, Avi pushes the portrayal of a feminist character further. It is not just her actions on board ship, not just her rejection of the socially prescribed female clothing and role that distinguish her. Rather, it is her daring choice of her own identity. Although Avi writes that Charlotte's "accept[ance of] the responsibility of wishing for (and crucially) doing what she wants" ("Seeing," 6) answers Morwenna, it also carries the potential to speak clearly to today's readers. Curiously enough in this age supposedly enlightened by feminist ideas, potential film producers found Charlotte's ending an undesirable one, inappropriate for a young audience (*Boston Globe*). Charlotte Doyle's "confession is the ultimate proof of her liberation" ("Seeing," 6), an affirmation of her self-defined and self-directed female identity that continues to threaten social mores and gender roles. Perhaps even more threatening to the adult world, however, is Avi's portrayal in a children's book of a child independent of thought and action, a child who dares to defy adults. Indeed, Avi charges his young audience with powerful truths.

7. Avi as Subverter and Antiauthoritarian

But as the stern and plain truth, even in the dress of this (in novels) much exalted race, was a part of the purpose of this book, I
will not, for these readers, abate one hole in the Dodger's coat, or
one scrap of curl-paper in the girl's dishevelled hair. I have no
faith in the delicacy which cannot bear to look upon them. I have
no desire to make proselytes among such people. I have no respect
for their opinion, good or bad; do not covet their approval; and do
not write for their amusement. I venture to say this without
reserve; for I am not aware of any writer in our language having a
respect for himself, or held in any respect by his posterity, who
ever has descended to the taste of this fastidious class.

—Charles Dickens, "Preface," *Oliver Twist*[1]

In "The Child in Literature" Avi speculates on the inherently
subversive nature of children's literature. Children's fiction "is
about unfairness, inconsistency, and lack of justice in the adult
world."[2] Avi's young characters fight for fairness and consistency;
they insist upon justice. This battle often places the child or
young adult against the adult world and, as with *The True Confessions of Charlotte Doyle*, presents young readers with literary
role models who assert control in adult spheres. The nonjock
characters in *S.O.R. Losers* try to appease the adults who push
them onto the soccer field and who promise them a winning team
if they just try hard enough; yet, the book ends in triumph when
the boys dismiss the adults and define success on their own
terms. Tony, the young sailor in *Windcatcher*, subverts by dis-
obeying his grandmother by pursuing sunken treasure, whereas

111

Owen, in *A Place Called Ugly*, at first simply defies his parents and escalates to challenge all levels of social authority. *Smuggler's Island* extends this antiauthoritarian behavior as Shadrach takes it upon himself to unburden his island home from the tyranny of smugglers. These books address "the question of control—parents, teachers, police—[as] absolutely fundamental" ("Child," 48) to children.

In a recent collection of short stories about growing up, Avi reconstructs elements of his own childhood to ground his piece about three nine-year-old boys in 1946 who quietly agree to undermine their scouting law. The main character in "Scout's Honor"[3] narrates the boys' journey from Brooklyn, New York, into Palisades, New Jersey, for an overnight stay. All three want to move up in the scouting ranks, but, even more, each boy needs to prove to himself that he is tough, at least as tough as his two companions. Violating the scouting pledge of honesty, each boy lies to his parents about the lack of adult supervision on the trip. The excursion itself proves disastrous: They forget other scouting guidelines; they eat too early or ruin their limited food supply; they arrive ill equipped to build appropriate shelter; the rain drenches them; they retreat to the shelter of home. The journey concludes with yet another lie as the boys agree to withhold from the Scoutmaster their failure to enjoy the overnight hike. The white lies constitute only minor breaches of authority; however, the boys' real subversive action lies in their concluding pact with each other. Knowing that the trip proves them not "loyal, helpful, friendly, courteous, kind, obedient, cheerful, thrifty, brave, clean, and reverent" ("Scout's," 126), they betray the very scout's honor invoked to seal the agreement. Their subversion thus stems from their self-knowledge and willingness to claim it.

S.O.R. Losers

The young boys in "Scout's Honor" have older counterparts in *S.O.R. Losers*. Although the novel comes close to Avi's personal experience, it remains a work of fiction. Avi gives to the narrator,

Ed Sitrow, his own last name, Wortis, spelled in reverse. The novel shares the episodic quality of the short story; "[s]hort, pithy chapters highlighting key events maintain the pace necessary for successful comedy."[4] Each chapter title leads the reader through the chronology of the story but with the good-humored hyperbole characteristic of the narrator. One can "hear" the chapter titles as if they were a sportscaster's colorful commentary during a game.

Action impels this novel, and rightly so given one reviewer's assessment of the book as "one of the funniest and most original sports sagas on record" (Burns, 49). The irony of the story unfolds when readers realize that even though action drives sports, these eleven nonjocks lack the basic skills and interest to sustain a dynamic game.

The paradoxical tone of the novel becomes one of its most subversive aspects. Satire provides first the narrator, then the reader, the opportunity to observe events and then to see them in a different perspective. Irony requires a skillful observer capable of uncovering incongruities. Ed Sitrow brings just the right combination of distance and involvement, of good humor and insight to narrate the story.

Sitrow, his buddy Saltz, and nine other seventh-graders have avoided all forms of sports throughout their education at South Orange Middle School. Accomplishments in art, writing, math, music, and more academic venues distinguish these eleven boys, who are finally tracked down and recruited to join the soccer team in the spirit of school tradition. Their history teacher, whose lack of skill as a coach matches their inability as players, articulates the adult reasoning:

> Mr. Lester's face made the ultimate transformation. He turned deathly white, and spoke as though from the grave. "S.O.R. believes in the whole person. We've created this team for your good. From now on you're going to play. Sports is a major part of American life. Starting tomorrow we've got a season to play. Six games. Let's do it with honor."[5]

These values clearly belong to an adult world that comes out in full force to support the boys and to practice with them. The school's parents, teachers, and administrators all believe that with enough cheerleading and preparation, the boys have the ability to win. The well-intended belief that if one tries hard enough, one can do anything quickly suffers distortion as the adults begin to advocate winning rather than merely playing the game well.

The team, itself, however, begins consciously to resist these values. Initially, although they do not want to play, they enter the field with resignation. As they experience astounding defeats against other teams, they begin to take pride in losing—they lose exceptionally well. Although the desire to salvage at least one win in the season seizes everyone else, team members start to question the meaning behind this push for success. When told that "it's important to win" (*S.O.R.*, 71), one team member can only respond with a simple "Why?" (*S.O.R.*, 71) The question goes unanswered, the motive proven suspect.

The question gains additional complexity when the team plays Parkville, the only other team with as dismal a record as theirs. The S.O.R. team notices the opposing team:

> The big difference was their faces. Stiff and tight. You could see, they *wanted* to win. Had to win. We were relaxed. Having a grand old time.
> Not them. (*S.O.R.*, 85–86)

If it is so important to win, why is there so little joy in the game, in the attempt to win? Even after the game, when Parkville has won and S.O.R. has lost again, they "hugged each other, screamed and hooted like teams do when they win championships. And we were a lot happier than those Parkville guys who had won" (*S.O.R.*, 89). If it is so important to win, then why is there so little joy in the victory?

The school's incessant rallying eventually energizes the team— with a commitment to maintain their losing streak, to become "champions of the bloody bottom" (*S.O.R.*, 89). They claim S.O.R. Loser as their slogan and add LOSERS to their team shirts. Although others condemn their action as defeatist, the boys comprehend the honesty and integrity of their slogan. They dare to undermine the authority that not only tells them to try but also pressures them to win. They challenge their parents, teachers, administrators, and those of their schoolmates who have ascribed to this false value to recognize their genuine achievements. The most rebellious element of all, however, is the team's insistence on their independence. Like Charlotte Doyle, they know themselves and adamantly choose to remain true to themselves; they even dare to celebrate themselves.

Even writing this kind of story becomes an insurgent act. In it, "the child is held up as a metaphor for unsocial behavior" ("Child," 47), and the author honors that behavior. The characters become role models; the author, antiauthoritarian.

Avi writes that "growing up means learning two key things: our possibilities and our limitations" ("Child," 46). The boys in "Scout's Honor" and the team members in *S.O.R. Losers* begin to discover their possibilities in light of society's imposed limitations. As the world of adults dictates rules, even those of the boy scout pledge or the rules of a soccer game, these boys recognize that their possibilities fall outside the expected, the prescribed limitations. Rather than dismissing themselves as rejected misfits, they claim their possibilities by defying society. For these characters as well as for Avi, who, "when . . . told [he] was a bad writer . . . [decided] to prove that [he] could write ("Scout's," 139), defiance motivates.

Windcatcher

Defiance in *Windcatcher* takes an initially mild form. Eleven-year-old Tony Souza wants to spend the money he has earned from his newspaper route on a motor scooter, but his father prefers that Tony save the $300. Because Tony values money for what it can purchase, he soon finds a way to spend the money that is more acceptable to his parents. They allow him to buy a small sailboat to take on his summer vacation to his grandmother's coastal Connecticut home on the condition that he complete sailing lessons and wear a life preserver. Although Tony's defiance is quite mild—he really only resists his father's suggestion to save the money—his particular purchase of a sailboat spurns restrictions. Sailing, Tony enjoys individual freedom. He sails alone, enjoying the independence.

> Leaving behind a gurgling wake, the *Snark* cut through the water effortlessly. Tony, with one hand on the sheet to keep the sail from blowing out, the other hand on the tiller, felt as if his whole body were humming. The silence sang. With a salt wind blowing in his face, he felt as if he could go on forever.
> "I love this!" he yelled.[6]

Tony loves the autonomy he experiences as a lone sailor. That liberty also accounts for why Tony enjoys spending time with his Grandma Souza, a self-sufficient woman living alone, who not only understands but also promotes Tony's need to separate from his parents and from authority figures. At first she encourages Tony to take small risks, such as eating a freshly dug clam raw; later, she colludes with him on searching for the rumored treasure from a sunken ship off the coast of Swallows Bay, his sailing territory.

Avi opens the novel with "[a]n introductory flashback describing a violent storm at sea and resultant shipwreck [that] quickly sets the tone for the bracing mystery adventure."[7] Finding the lost ship, *Swallow,* grows into an obsession with Tony as he increasingly believes that the name of Money Island, off which the ship is supposed to have sunk, proves the existence of a valuable sunken treasure. He and his grandmother research the ship and its supposed captain Ezra Littlejohn, whose statue in town faces out to sea. The circumstance of having his grandfather's model ship in his room leads Tony to discover that Littlejohn carved the ship model and was not the ship's captain but rather its quartermaster. Furthermore, the lens Tony finds on the floor of the model cabin leads him to believe that the spyglass in the statue's hand points to the *Swallow*'s shipwreck and its treasure.

Tony never really exhibits mastery as a detective. Although intuitively and cleverly piecing together disparate elements of the mystery, Tony fails to envision a whole solution. Unlike Chris in *No More Magic,* Tony never learns to ask the right questions. His information remains incomplete, although his hunches prove lucky and somewhat dangerous. As Tony sails Swallows Bay in search of the shipwreck, he also spies on a man and a woman. His sailing instructor, Chris, tells him they are diving for treasure. He pursues the couple a number of times until finally they tell him to stay away from them. In keeping with his defiant spirit, Tony does not comply even when they use their motorboat to capsize his sailboat—a direct threat. Tony "had no doubts that those people were trying to frighten him. In part they had succeeded. But they had also made him more determined than ever to find out what it was they wanted so much to hide" (*Windcatcher*, 62).Tony continues to follow them and, ultimately, is "captured" by them.

Tony's pursuit of the couple echoes *Man from the Sky* as both boys observe and eventually interrupt illegal adult activity. Like Tony, the adults act subversively. As he disobeys his grandmother, they disobey the state order protecting sunken cargo. Even though they both revolt against authority, Tony resolves his moral conflict in satisfying ways. The desire for money pulls him forward. However, when the couple offers him half of their find, potentially thousands of dollars, he refuses, choosing instead to expose them to the proper authorities.

Reviewer Hazel Rochman writes that the "sailing lore will attract readers, as will the good humor of the story, the characters, and the moral conflict."[8] Ultimately, Tony claims the independence, the freedom, and the fun of sailing. He asks his grandmother's permission to stay for the remainder of the summer, not to continue to look for submerged treasures but instead to "catch the wind" (*Windcatcher*, 124). As Tony discloses his reason for sailing, he reveals a rejection of adult materialism. He learns that money cannot buy everything. It cannot purchase the exhilaration of sailing or the self-sufficiency he earned and enjoys. Even though Tony's morally correct choice signals a new maturity and movement into adulthood, his decision to sail for pure pleasure subverts as it celebrates the emancipation of childhood.

A Place Called Ugly

Owen Coughlin attempts to hold on to his childhood in *A Place Called Ugly*, the subversive act of an adolescent "David fighting the Goliaths of change."[9] This desire places him in direct conflict with numerous adult authorities: his parents, the town's legal system, wealthy entrepreneurs, and local townspeople. Avi chooses summer as the temporal setting for the story, a time that exemplifies the idyllic nature of childhood, a time full of seemingly endless days, a time when families are together in ways uncharacteristic of other seasons, and a time adults tend to recall when asked to remember something about their childhoods.

For 14-year-old Owen, summer places him between the spring of his childhood and the apparent winter of adolescence. He reflects on his summers as times of family unity. During the summer, his older brother and sister traditionally join him and their parents on Grenlow's Island, and the family shares a unique sense of wholeness. Owen reminisces about the prior summer when he was 13 and for the first time his 19-year-old brother, Pete, and 20-year-old sister, Alice, do not take this vacation. Initially, "[b]eing without them seemed wrong, as if something had been forgotten."[10] Clearly, what has been forgotten is Owen, and what is wrong is that Owen feels alone. He tries to celebrate that aloneness.

> "Alone!" he shouted back at the sky. This time he threw it out loud, hard, telling himself that lasting the longest meant you won the race. To be alone meant you won.
> "Alone!" he shouted again and again and again. "Alone. . . ."
> (*Place*, 11)

His shouts to the air remain somewhat empty and unheard. At this early point in the novel, Owen looks toward solitariness and panics, the same reaction that he feels at 14 at having been left alone by his parents. As the novel progresses, Owen realizes the power of solitude and starts to leave behind the desperation of loneliness. He chooses to be alone, to stay at the summer cottage and protect it from demolition. He chooses the detachment, the elusiveness, serenity, and independence of the lone heron he discovered in a marsh when he was seven. Like Maggie in *The Blue Heron*, he "wanted to touch it, to capture it, to bring it home and keep it forever" (*Place*, 21). The bird has the ability to make Owen forget his fears; it heralds aloneness as an empowering position.

Summer also represents to Owen a time of stasis, a time of welcome continuity that contrasts with the rest of his transient life. With his father's promotions, his family moves frequently. The most reliable constant in Owen's life has been the summer cottage on isolated Grenlow's Island, The island itself serves as a metaphor: It is an isolated place whole unto itself; it projects a feeling of permanence—it continues on even as visitors arrive and depart; self-sufficiency characterizes the island inhabitants. On his second day of chosen isolation at the cottage, Owen recalls his sixth summer there. At the age of 10, he methodically, meticulously builds elaborate sand castles. "Castle after castle went up. He kept thinking they all might topple, collapse, or just melt away. It didn't happen. They became more than castles. They became a city—a world" (*Place*, 40). Owen does not consider the inevitability of the castles' destruction and fights with hopeless urgency to save his world from destruction by the tide. Owen wants things to stay the same; he wants his city, his world to hold still.

Until he fixes his location, Owen cannot stabilize his identity. His decision to stay on the island becomes an attempt to know who he is. The only sure identity Owen has had is the one developed during 10 years of 3 weeks in August with his family in the cottage. The razing of the cottage in order to construct a summer resort threatens the only place in which Owen has known himself. He himself does not command this knowledge until the novel's end. Taking a relatively safe antiauthoritarian stand, he refuses to return home with his parents. As with the sand castles, Owen's father calls him in and tells him to stop acting so foolishly. Still, his parents allow him to stay, tell others in town to look after him, and leave him some money and clothes. Owen tests these limits when he decides to stay on and see the demolition battle through to its conclusion. As long as his parents set the boundaries to his defiance, the action becomes theirs, not his. His identity remains ill formed—or formed only by their perception of him. Only when Owen decides to stay and oppose the house's eradication does he also seize control over himself. Symbolically, the house represents his childhood, and staying reveals his desire to remain a child. Directing the house's destruction, therefore, also means Owen takes command of his childhood and chooses when to leave it behind to enter adolescence—and even adulthood.

> When I understood [that the house was a memory], I finally understood why I loved the place so much. It was because of all the memories, memories that each year promised summers yet to come. The house was the place—for me—where everything began again and again and again. Having that place, that past, gave me a future. (*Place*, 129)

Because he will always have it as a memory, he can leave childhood behind. Once he understands that the memories are intangible by nature, he can let go of their tangible representation, the house. Once Owen finally makes the connection between the past, the present, and the future, he is able to claim the past as memory in the present and enter the future with confidence.

Avi's "skillfully constructed story [that] alternates between the present and the past presented in flashbacks, printed in italics and set in an irregular sequence, make[s the] parallel relationships obvious."[11] Readers can interpret the narrative structure's slow revelation of Owen's identity. Owen disobeys his parents to stay on the island and to protect the house from demolition without really knowing why. Yes, he knows he wants to save the house, but he does not understand the intensity of his emotion, nor does he comprehend his motivation. In tracing the interaction of past and present, readers develop an understanding of Owen's complexity. Readers come to see the deep rooted motivation for his subversive actions.

As Owen spends time on the island resisting the hotel development, he also begins to see the island's year-round residents in a different light. In one flashback, Owen recalls a befuddling incident from a few years past. Yearning to try on a new baseball mitt Owen received as a birthday gift from his father, the island storekeeper's son, Bill Janick, allows himself to play pitch-and-catch with the younger Owen. Bill catches, Owen pitches.

> Owen threw the ball wild. High over Bill's head it sailed, landing way down the road. Disgusted, Bill stood with his hands on his hips, looking after it. Owen, not sure what to do, waited for Bill to get it.
> Suddenly Bill turned on him. "What you waiting for?" he snapped.
> "The ball," said Owen.
> "Look, kid," said Bill. "I'm not behind the counter now. Fetch your own stuff."
> Slowly, Owen walked to where the ball lay. When he returned, Bill had gone . . . Bill was nowhere to be seen. But all the way home Owen kept trying to understand why Bill had been angry with him. (*Place*, 29–30)

The child grasps only the differences between the boys' ages; faced with Bill's reaction based on the differences in their socioeconomic class, Owen is confused. That Owen recalls this episode from his past suggests that these differences still elude him. In Terri Janick, Bill's younger sister, Owen finds a confidante and friend who listens to his desire to protect the house. Bill and Owen have an altercation in the present, this time over Terri. Not only does Bill warn Owen to stay away from her but he also stresses again the difference in their class status. To the islanders, Owen can be only an outsider, one of those summer visitors whose spending enables the permanent residents to subsist over the winter. In protecting the house, Owen again assumes his privilege and selfishly acts out of it. Owen gains some comprehension of class differences when he visits Miss Devlin, the wealthy entrepreneur sponsoring the hotel construction. Although he perceives the social distance between them, he still does not acquire insight into the islanders' stake in the hotel; he continues to fight because of his own feelings about the house. However, his battles meet with tremendous resistance from the townspeople, including Miss Devlin and Terri. Only after Owen realizes what the house means to him can he begin to consider what it means to others. Still, he remembers what Miss Devlin tells him about the economic promise of the hotel, and he recalls what Terri shares with him about the hotel as a way she can escape from the island. He patches together the various pieces of information in an important revelation:

> Maybe I had been wrong—wrong to my parents, wrong to the island people, wrong to Terri, wrong to keep them from the summers *they* so desperately wanted, needed, had to have. They didn't have my memories. To get them, they had to take the house away, put it aside, bury it under the promise of the hotel. Maybe they did need that. Maybe it was their only hope.
> I didn't have to have hope. (*Place*, 129)

Like the narrative structure, Owen's ability to move between the past, the present, and the future, and his final ability to make connections between the three, justifies his subversive acts. Owen climbs the house and finishes painting it, decorating it with "a picture of the universe, *my* universe, the way I wanted things to be" (*Place*, 115). Owen defies those who declare the house ugly and paints it his version of "beautiful—alive, sparkling, and glowing" (*Place*, 121). After Owen lets go of the house, he looks at it again with an understanding that speaks to his newfound identity: "The house was beautiful. And maybe, just maybe, so was I" (*Place*, 130). Now that he knows himself, Owen defies authority once more as he takes control of the demolition; the bulldozer stands at the ready, but Owen acting alone implodes the house.

Just before the countdown, his mother tells him that " 'Grownups know when to forget. Kids don't. Kids won't let go' " (*Place*, 126). The final image in the novel shows Owen weeping for his lost childhood, yet holding onto his memories. He may have let go, but he vows not to forget. Like the characters in *S.O.R. Losers* and *Windcatcher*, Owen subverts the expected call into adulthood and begins his entry on his own terms—with a celebratory reclamation of childhood.

Shadrach's Crossing

In *Shadrach's Crossing* (reissued in paperback as *Smuggler's Island*), Avi again exalts the genuine force of childhood. At 12, Shadrach Faherty does not know—and does not care to know—when to let go. Rather than taming Shad's tenacity, Avi subverts as he enables Shad's perseverance to effect real change throughout the society. Avi fills this main character with a preteen-ager's pure, unambiguous belief in right against wrong, a belief that charges Shad's moral outrage and that demands action.

Once again, Avi sets the novel in a historical period: on an island during the Prohibition in 1932. The historical setting serves as more than a backdrop to Shad's story. With the lines between adult and child clearly drawn, the scene directly influences his character and accents the rigidity of his society. In the Depression, a time threatening childhood, Shad's parents eagerly work to protect him, to afford to Shad and his younger brother, Brian, some semblance of a worry-free, enjoyable childhood. The impoverished community on Lucker's Island suffers additional privation during the Depression. A boat-motor mechanic, Shad's father has difficulty finding work on the 40-person island whose primary industry as a port can sustain itself only by the illegal trafficking of alcohol. Avi describes the poverty in personal as well as communal terms but always through Shadrach's perspective. Shadrach looks at his mother and sees that "[s]he was younger than his father, but looked older. Her mouth was thin and tight, as was her body. Her teeth were poor, her hair streaked with grey, her arms and hands covered with freckles. The dress she wore, once brightly checked in red and blue, had faded so much that only a vague pattern of lines could be seen."[12] Shad recognizes the marks of their poverty in his mother's demeanor as well as in her clothing. He sees her as pitiful and helpless. As Shad wanders through the town, he notices its poverty, too. "Most of the houses were abandoned. It always amazed Shad how quickly, how quietly the empty houses fell apart. First the windows went. Then the doors. Roofs sagged. Walls shrank, split, turned colorless as they caved in. The only thing left behind was silence" (*Shadrach*, 40).

The historical setting sharpens the contrast between the haves and the have-nots on the island. Unlike Owen, whose privilege allows him the luxury of a relatively late awakening to differences in socioeconomic class, Shad faces the differences daily.

> Twenty or so houses lay scattered. Empty. Still. Broken.
>
> Except for one house. It was the house where Kinlow stayed when he was on the island. Though Kinlow only came on Sundays and left Tuesdays, people always avoided the area.
>
> Kinlow's house wasn't a new one. But it wasn't broken down either. (*Shadrach*, 40–41)

When Nevill arrives on the island in his boat, *The Vole*, Shad compares the craft with other boats he knows. "*The Vole* looked to be about sixty feet in length, painted cream white with gold trim. Its cabin was varnished teak that glistened in the sun. A fancy boat, thought Shad, a rich man's boat" (*Shadrach*, 36). Shad's judgments about what people own lead him immediately to make judgments about who people are. If they do not have money, then they belong to the community and they are desperate. However, like Kinlow and Nevill, those who possess nice houses or boats remain outsiders to the community. Shad extends his knowledge that Kinlow's money came from his extensive smuggling operation to the assumption that Nevill's "rich man's boat" marks Nevill as a smuggler, too.

In this mystery form, Avi provides his readers with more information than he does his characters. Avi insists that readers question Shad's judgments about a person's morality based upon their appearance. Shad makes a mistake in his estimation of Sheraton, whose binoculars, "splendid, bound in black leather, with shiny brass metal bands" (*Shadrach*, 50), impress Shad. "As the reader will guess on the instant, [Nevill and Sheraton] are the opposite of what they seem to Shad. . . ."[13]

Shad discerns that "[t]he smugglers' activities sustain the islanders' precarious economy and make it possible for them to continue living there in spite of the increasingly hard times."[14]

However, that understanding includes no room for forgiveness—neither for Kinlow for organizing the illicit activity nor for the islanders nor for his parents for participating in it. Just as Shad's resolute morality misleads his appraisals of Nevill and Sheraton, it also provokes him to poison the corruption.

Reviews of this book place it in the mystery genre. Even though one review states that the "plotting won't get Avi a passing grade in mystery circles" (*Kirkus*, 662), other reviews praise the "realistic novel of suspense . . . [whose] [t]ension runs high from the very beginning, made so by short, pithy sentences, curt dialogue, superb pacing, and plenty of action" (*Dictionary*, 590–91). Shad creates the tension and it belongs to him. The tautness of the novel stems from Avi's portrayal of Shad as a boy willingly defying his society with the declared intention of undoing that culture. Young readers especially know the dangers of going against adult mores, rules, and expectations; they experience the anxiety of Shad's risk taking. In fact, "although the plot's twists and surprises maintain suspense to the very end, the book is less an adventure story than a novel about a boy's refusal to give in. . . ."[15]

Authority wears many faces in *Shadrach's Crossing*. If the law stands as the highest authority, then Kinlow breaks that law with his alcohol-smuggling operation. Kinlow, however, holds power over the people on the island: They need to participate in the illegal activity in order to survive, so Kinlow, rather than the government, functions as their authority. Shad is accountable to all levels of authority, beginning with his parents but ultimately ending with his own morality. Therefore, when rebelling against authority, Shad acts out of personal conviction. Finding the adult world disappointing, hopeless, and untrustworthy, he trusts only himself.

Shad's actions first take the form of disobedience against his parents, the first level of a young person's subversion. Shad's father comprehends the evil and danger of Kinlow. At various points throughout the novel, he forbids Shad to break curfew and tells Shad to avoid Kinlow and his men. As Shad's transgressions escalate, so does his father's sense of protectiveness and, with that, the seriousness of his discipline. As Shad becomes more determined to disable Kinlow and to restore pride to the town, his father becomes more resolved to save Shad from peril. Son and father clash after Shad confesses to invading Kinlow's house. Mr. Faherty makes good on his earlier threat to whip Shad into obedience.

> Shad moved across the room, took the belt from the nail in the wall, came back and handed it over. Mr. Faherty took it, studied it as it lay across his still-dirty fingers. Shad backed off to the opposite side of the room, as far away from his father as he could get.
> "It's for you," his father said. "For your own good. You don't listen to me. You never do. You're putting all of us in a bad way. I'm not backing down this time." The belt, dangling from his hand, just touched the floor. "I'm the one that takes care of you. Me and your mother. We're in charge."
> "Prove it," said Shad, only to be instantly sorry he had spoken. (*Shadrach*, 85)

Despite his father's insistence that he heads the family, the scene concludes with Mr. Faherty's transferal of moral fortitude and its obligation to Shad. The father never takes the disciplinary action he threatens, and Shad reminds him of past instances of his inaction, exposing his impotence as a father and as a morally responsible man.

Ironically, although his father no longer poses a physical obstacle to Shadrach, his father's inaction daunts Shad. "He had won out over his father. But the more he thought about it the clearer it became that he hadn't really wanted to. If his father was so helpless, if his parents couldn't do anything, either of them, not even to him, their son, how could he, Shad, think of doing something to Kinlow?" (*Shadrach*, 89–90) More than anything, Shad yearns for adults to act like adults. He fights against a system, Kinlow's system, which collapsed the roles of child and adult; because the adults fail to assume the mantle, Shad takes on the adult role of crusader for justice.

Yet, Shad goes about his work in a distinctly childlike fashion. He spies and eavesdrops; he navigates the town by foot through its labyrinthine connection of paths and backyards traversed by kids, who prefer them to the main roads for adult vehicles. He tries to enlist the help of his best friend, Davey, whose own fright prevents him from joining Shad. Finally, he accepts the help of his brother Brian—the only bit of companionship offered to him. All the appropriate childlike emotions accompany him: At times he feels frightened, helpless, and alone. In true adult fashion, however, Shad notices these emotions and perseveres in his quest without indulging them. Despite his lack of confidence in his parents, he continues to reach out for adult help, which eventually arrives in the shape of a well-meaning ferryman who helps them escape from Kinlow's capture. "Readers might be puzzled by the . . . portrayal of the Coast Guard, who seem rather timid and unknowledgeable in the ways of catching smugglers red-handed: Shad, with his shrewdness and stubborn courage, outshines them by far."[16] The failure of the Coast Guard, in the form of Nevill, has less to do with their incompetence and more to do with Shad's miscalculation about Nevill. Further, with the peculiarly strong conviction of his youth, Shad shuts out all adults as untrustworthy.

Avi does not end the novel simply with the capture of the bad guys. Kinlow and his gang are arrested, but Shad exacts a different kind of justice. Keeping wholly in character by adhering to the strict morality that fueled his outrage and again displaying immature attributes, Shad insists that Kinlow apologize to the Fahertys, a microcosm of the larger island community. Even as Kinlow discounts the importance of the apology, he finds it difficult to deliver—and the community, shamed that a child did what they could not do, falls silent at the apology. Now Shad can abandon his adult role. Unlike Owen, his letting go allows him to ask to be a child.

> "And you're all right now?" his mother asked.
> Again Shad nodded. He just stood there, not knowing what to do, all but overwhelmed by a wave of dizziness that swept over him. Then the tide he had kept down for so long could no longer be contained. With a half-stagger, half-leap, he threw himself up against his parents. He could feel their arms, Brian's arms, hugging him, holding him. (*Shadrach*, 178)

In "The Child in Literature," Avi insightfully recognizes that

> Children's literature, in the deepest sense, most often tells
> the tale of the acquisition of knowledge, but it is knowledge
> which in itself brings about—by fact or metaphor—the end of
> childhood. These triumphant endings, by virtue of the fact that
> they usher the child into adulthood, are, ironically, a kind of
> defeat. This is because, more often than not, these endings con-
> stitute an end to idealism. Children's literature often seems to
> be saying to children, "Don't do what we have done. Do better.
> Please make the world into what I, like you, once believed it
> capable of becoming. Don't make the mistake I made. Don't
> grow up."
> . . . But wait! There is a "subversive" children's literature,
> a literature in which the protagonist does not go back home,
> but rather leaves home. *Escapes* might be the better word.
> ("Child," 49)

Clearly, all four of these novels meet Avi's definition of children's
literature that subverts. *S.O.R. Losers* concludes with young
adult characters who reject the adult measures of success. These
young men find no comfort in returning to an adult world that
demands a false heroism; rather, they escape into a self-definition
inclusive of their inadequacies as well as their strengths. Tony, in
Windcatcher, chooses not to return home but instead stays with
his grandmother; he acquires the knowledge necessary to escape
further into the freedoms of childhood. *A Place Called Ugly* finds
Owen returning to his parents only after destroying—leaving to
the realm of memory—his true home on the island. Like
Shadrach, he grips tenaciously the idealism necessary to change
the adult world; Shadrach sheds the adult world in order to discover a childhood. In an interview, Avi states that he writes about
kids "caught up in a situation essentially created by adults."[17] In
these books and in many others, Avi places his characters in situ-
ations that demand that they act in antiauthoritarian ways in
order to overcome their victimization. The subversiveness of Avi's
children's literature stems from his appreciation that adulthood
restrains and entraps. It may not be the place to help children
enter but the place from which to assist their escape.

8. Avi as Family Auteur

All happy families are like one another; each unhappy family is
unhappy in its own way.

—Leo Tolstoy, *Anna Karenina*[1]

The family, as the place in which a young person's identity is first
formed and tested, appears as a consistent thread in Avi's fiction
for children and young adults. In much of his work, the traditional nuclear family of mother, father, and children serves as a
stable background. In novels such as *No More Magic, Who Stole
the Wizard of Oz?, Who Was That Masked Man, Anyway?, Smugglers' Island,* and *Something Upstairs,* Avi casts parents in supportive roles; they provide information necessary to the main
characters when asked, but the children and young adults hold
center stage in these narratives. Avi shifts the family composition
somewhat when he writes about divorced families. In *Sometimes I
Think I Hear My Name* and *Blue Heron,* Conrad and Maggie each
live in a family separated by divorce. However, even in these por-
trayals, Avi does not abandon the possibility of a nuclear family.
Conrad's relationship with his aunt and uncle replicates the traditional mother-father-child structure. Conrad himself actively
seeks to know his biological parents better; Maggie strives to
become part of her father's second family, with his new wife and
new baby.

Of course, the family has changed over time, and sociologists
and historians now begin to understand the nuclear family as
both a luxury and a myth.[2] So, too, does Avi question the likeli-
hood of the traditional family. In *The True Confessions of Char-*

129

lotte Doyle, Avi's heroine decidedly rejects this conventional unit as restrictive and incompatible with her hard-won identity. Three recent books, *Punch with Judy*, *The Barn*, and *Beyond the Western Sea. Book One: The Escape from Home*, examine various permutations of the nuclear family. In these books, the central relationships between siblings take precedence over relationships with parents. The three novels play on and fracture familial patterns seen elsewhere in Avi's work. They speak in a voice more reflective and somber than in other books, one tinged with loss—especially of parents—but sustained by hope—embodied in lifelong ties to siblings. By placing the stories in historical settings, from 1850 to 1870, Avi suggests that the rending of the nuclear family may be a phenomenon not unique to contemporary times.

Punch with Judy

In *Punch with Judy* Avi turns to theatrical influences to expand the definition of family. The novel introduces a traveling troupe of circus-type performers: acrobat Blodger, juggler Twig, animal trainer Zun, medicine man Doc, contortionist Molly McSneed, showman Joe McSneed, and the McSneed's equestrian daughter, Judy. Joe McSneed brings home and in essence adopts a nameless, homeless, eight-year-old orphan to complete his performance family. McSneed decides "to call him—Punch" and thus anticipates the theatrical future of this band of "Merry Men."

Punch remains an outsider to the troupe, however. Mr. McSneed provides him with a job and, to that extent, an identity. Nevertheless, without a full-fledged family, this identity remains cast in negatives: Punch does not become part of the act, "nor did he lose his limp, learn to stand very tall, nor manage to look anyone in the eye,"[3] nor does he become integrated into the family. In some ways, Mr. McSneed acts as a father to Punch. On the street he finds him dancing a pitiful, yet humorous jig. Later he defends and protects Punch against accusations from the troupe, allowing Punch to stay connected to them even though he feels no sense of belonging. The dollar coin Mr. McSneed gives Punch as a reward for his street jig becomes Punch's inheritance; the coin becomes a family legacy when, at the novel's end, Punch gives it to Judy. In a way in which fathers often view their sons, Mr. McSneed sees in Punch the future of his family. He calls him his "insurance policy" (*Punch*, 8) and on his deathbed confides to Judy his expectations that Punch will carry on their troupe.

Readers are never quite sure how Mr. McSneed feels about Punch nor, for that matter, how Punch views Mr. McSneed. Avi maintains a distant narrative voice here, one "removed from any involvement, any sense of warm presence."[4] That voice prohibits readers from knowing the emotions and attitudes of the characters; instead, it serves "to have the reader experience as the audience would a medicine show."[5] Therefore, as in drama, characters can be assessed only by their actions. Mr. McSneed sees in Punch the potential for making money. However, Mr. McSneed also acts like Punch's father to such an extent that when he dies, Punch is once again orphaned, in effect.

Mr. McSneed, also referred to as Da, could be considered the head of the entire company-family. They all claim to love him through both the prosperous and the more recently trying times. After Da's death, family members vie for position as new leader.

> During these four years [when the troupe traveled under Da's supervision], Mrs. McSneed never developed a liking for the boy. Not that she abused him; she just never took him to heart. Regarding Twig, Blodger, Doc, and Zun, they were more active in their dislike, flinging frowns—and now and again a kick—his way. (*Punch*, 13)

Mrs. McSneed and others see the family as intact and not in need of another child. Punch's desire to attend Da's funeral is dismissed quickly: " 'Who cares bug's breath for Punch?' Twig sneered." Turning to Judy, he exhorts, "You're Da's kid, not him" (*Punch*, 22). Punch remains marginalized in the troupe and in the family.

Judy proves the linchpin to Punch's acceptance. Initially, she obeys her father and treats Punch as something of a friend. "[T]he two played together (Punch was the follower), talked together (Punch was the listener), ate together (Punch brought the food)" (*Punch*, 14–15). Even Da provided Judy with contradictory messages about the relationship he intended her to have with Punch. He instructs her to be Punch's friend and then intimates that they might have a more involved relationship: " 'Judy, love, be fair; will you be wanting to tramp with your parents for the whole of your life?' " (*Punch*, 14) On his deathbed, Da further confuses Judy's relationship with Punch as he confides in her his desire for Punch to assume with her responsibilities for the troupe when he comes of age. Thus, Da directs Judy to act as friend, perhaps wife, then sister to Punch.

Following Da's death, Judy's actions toward Punch demonstrate her confusion and ambivalence about just which role she should play with him. At the funeral, "she tugged at him and made him sit at her side in the first pew. That was pleasure" (*Punch*, 26); yet, when leaving the funeral, "Punch touched Judy's hand. She pushed it away. That was pain" (*Punch*, 27). She moves first toward and then away from him. More than anything, she wants Punch to begin assuming the responsibilities she knows will be placed upon him. She urges him to make decisions for himself, to stop relying on her. When Horatio, New Moosup's parson's son, leaves town with the troupe while being pursued by Sheriff Oxnard, Judy's feelings toward Punch become somewhat clearer. She sees Horatio as capable, self-sufficient, and loving. He relieves some of the intense responsibility for others that fell to her after Da's death. Horatio supports Judy in her struggle with her mad mother, who no longer recognizes her daughter. Seen as a rival by Punch, Horatio knows how to use Punch's affection for Judy to do what Judy wants him to do: to be funny on stage. A stranger to laughter, Horatio, "shaded to the dull side of life" (*Punch*, 112), finds relief from his father's sobriety in McSneed's "Merry Men." By novel's end, Judy orders her family constellation with clarity: With Punch's help, her mother accepts her again; she marries Horatio, who fills the role of husband; that action relegates Punch to the part of brother and coexecutor of her dying father's will. Daughter, wife, and sister, Judy even finds a place, an abandoned house that they take first as stage then as home to promote the stability of this transient family.

In *Punch with Judy*, Avi "explor[es] the tragic aspects of comedy"[6] primarily through the character of Punch. Punch first appears in the novel as Mr. McSneed's discovery, a tragic character indeed.

> One raw day in 1870—five years after the Civil War—a man
> came upon a boy. The man's face was round and ruddy, with
> blue eyes which fairly sparked laughs upon the world. The boy
> was pale and scrawny, with eyes barely able to steal glances.
> The man wore new boots. The boy's bare feet were caked with
> mud. The man's purple coat was warm. The boy shivered in
> rags. And it was a rakish top hat which sat on the man's head,
> whereas the boy had placed his hat—an old cloth one—on the
> muddy ground before him. For he was begging pennies by per-
> forming a shuffle of timid twists, jittery jumps, and sudden
> stops. The cap, however, was empty. (*Punch*, 1)

Punch is introduced without name, without origin, without identity. Avi gives him life by describing him in contrast to McSneed rather than on his own terms. Punch has no terms, only a memory "vague and very old. There was a family. And war. And an explosion. The vision vanished, leaving him with only a limp" (*Punch*, 115). Even though McSneed names him, Punch's individual identity eludes him until he also has a place, a location to call his own. The memory of a past family consciously returns to Punch only when the traveling troubadours find a house to possess as their own.

Avi breaks the novel into three parts: Part 1 concludes with Da's death, and part 2 ends with the departure of Doc, Blodger, and Zun. A sense of abandonment punctuates the novel and influences Punch's evolving self. Once he takes his place within the newly constructed show, he also gains a sense of self. In the first four years with the "Merry Men," all Punch earns is a name and a role. On moving into the house in Farktwist, he sees his relationships more clearly, although his identity is still based more on contrasts to than similarities with others. After Judy's marriage to Horatio, Punch mourns his inability to be her husband. Judy then confides to Punch Da's dying revelation that he intended them to share the show. This conversation closes one door and opens another to Punch: He cannot be Judy's husband, but he will be her partner. Judy further defines the association for Punch as she declares her love for him as a brother. This assertion gives Punch a place in the family, thus freeing him from the confinements of outsider; Judy welcomes Punch into the center of the family from his original position on its margin. Punch's new-found status and freedom "gave him such a sense of light and joy, such giddiness, that it set the very tips of his fingers to tingling" (*Punch*, 155). More importantly, that joy inspires Punch to act, to be genuinely funny in Twig's fresh orchestration of the show. Punch emerges not just as central to the family but also as key to the show itself.

The release of laughter decisively signals the troupe's release from Da. As the sheriff and his deputies guffaw, each of the remaining characters appear on stage to participate in the hilarity. First Twig, then Horatio, then Alexander the pig enter. When Mrs. McSneed "staggered out the door . . . 'Laughter!' she cried, lifting her arms toward heaven. 'My king has returned!' " (*Punch*, 163) Mirth, which had died with Da, reappears with Punch. No longer "[i]n a land where there is no laughter" (*Punch*, 39), the family has found a home—a home where merriment eases the pain, a home where emotions are felt.

Contrasts continue to define Punch. "[K]nowing that Judy's painful blows [in the 'Punch with Judy' show] were the cause of the sheriff's laughter and that this laughter meant liberation, that the more she struck him, the more free he was, why, he laughed with joy even as he cried with pain . . ." (*Punch*, 162). Pleasure and pain characterize Punch just as comedy comple-ments tragedy. At the end of his story, Punch grasps additional self-knowledge. Not only can he successfully transform the pain of tragedy into comic expression but also he knows he is good at doing so. Safe in a home, safe within a family, safe in an identity, "safe in [his] soul" (*Punch*, 111), Punch can now play—rather than be—someone else's fool.

The Barn

Avi's work itself seems a study of contrasts. From the mixed notices that struggled to understand *Punch with Judy* within various literary genres and within Avi's body of work, strong reviews greeted *The Barn*. Although *The Barn* fits nicely into the concise category of realistic historical fiction, it appears atypical of Avi's oeuvre. Not a textured high adventure story in the vein of *The True Confessions of Charlotte Doyle*, not a thematically charged re-visioning of history like *The Fighting Ground*, not a tensely calibrated mystery like *The Man Who Was Poe*, not an experiment in fiction like *Nothing but the Truth*, *The Barn* is a "small, beautiful historical novel [with] a timeless simplicity. It's the best thing he's done. Like MacLachlan's *Sarah, Plain and Tall* (1985), the story reaches from home to the universe."[7]

A microcosm of the universe, this family without a surname lives on a 300-acre claim in Yamhill County, Oregon, in 1855. "Although most children's books about the Oregon Trail recount the tremendous physical obstacles that the pioneers surmounted, *The Barn* is a contemplative survival story of a different sort."[8] The family endures because their physical isolation from others heightens the intensity of their relationships with each other. Nettie, 15, Harrison, 13, and Ben, 9, feel their universe constricting even more when their father "suffer[s] a fit of palsy."[9] Already having lost their mother to diphtheria, the interdependence of these children must increase if they are first to survive, second to hold onto the family land claim.

The novel opens with Nettie's retrieval of Ben from his boarding school in Portland, a place to which Father sends him because Ben is "fit for more than farming" (*Barn*, 2). Seventy years later, Ben reflects and recounts. Where Avi writes *Punch with Judy* in broad strokes and flamboyant language, he concentrates language here. Ben's spare narration grows organically from the time, the place, and the family. Although book-smart, Ben speaks with clarity in common language. Yet Avi conveys his genuine intelligence in disciplined, textured descriptions. Upon seeing his brother again after seven months, Ben thinks:

> How I envied his size and strength, his shovel-wide face and those hands as tough as horn. But though Harrison was as big as I was small, his eyes were like a deer's always seeming to ask permission. (*Barn*, 11)

And, when he first sees his father again after he suffers a stroke, Ben compares him to his memory.

> He lay on the big bed, back propped against the wall. He was fully dressed—faded blue-striped flannel shirt, wool trousers— though his boots were off. His hard hands lay by his sides like soft slabs of clay.
>
> The last time I had seen him, he was tall and strong. The only thing he'd never owed money on, he'd say, was his handsome face, and Mother bought it right off the shelf.
>
> Now that same face showed nothing but sick and sour dirtiness. His beard—about which he'd been so vain and about which I'd teased him often in fun—was all crossways, as was his grey-streaked hair.
>
> He made me think of an old corn husk doll without stuffing. As I stood staring, he made fluttering motions at the coverlet, his fingers jumping like small fish hauled to land. (*Barn*, 15)

Observant and attentive to detail, Ben uses speech formed by his everyday life. He does not labor over an image; rather he creates effective metaphors from familiar references. Both descriptions focus on hands; now Harrison's hard hands work the land whereas Father's lay useless, occasionally succumbing to uncontrollable spasms. Harrison takes on the mantle of work and responsibility his father can no longer bear. Ben's portrait of Father provides an inkling of the man-who-was even as it introduces the limitations of the man-who-is. It quietly reveals Father's key attributes: handsome, vain, and with a spirited sense of humor, all now broken. It speaks of an ordered although poor family who dresses appropriately and who takes pride in appearance.

The descriptions of these two familial relationships also bare essential information about Ben. He feels physically inadequate to assume the role of his brother, Harrison, even as he recognizes the incongruity of Harrison's timidity. Ben respects the physical strength he sees in his brother as he mourns the loss of that ability in his weakened father. Won over by his father's engaging face, he also shares in his sense of humor and his easy, joking manner. The nine-year-old sees his father as a pal, whereas, at 79, Ben recognizes that Father often jokes to cover flaws in his character. Even while wisecracking about his vanity, Father lightly acknowledges the family's indebtedness and suggests his failure.

Published in the year of Avi's own father's death, *The Barn* places Father at the center of this nuclear family, then examines what happens when Father can no longer provide for or hold the family together. In the rightful order of life, each child will endure the loss of both parents, and yet families persist—how? Harrison, Nettie, and Ben draw strength from their father and from each other. Avi conveys their individual complexities even as he demonstrates their joined commitment to hold the family together. Harrison brings physical strength and practical knowledge about farming and building. Harrison works hard and well with his sister Nettie, and he displays a tender streak when he carves a hinged box for her 16th birthday. They restrain from calling Ben until absolutely necessary, until the effort to maintain the farm and care for Father overwhelms them. Nettie keeps the family grounded. Level-headed, she knows she will not be with this family forever. And, even though she initially resists it because it does not make pragmatic sense, Nettie, too, comes to believe in and work to realize Ben's hopes for the barn.

Ben's position in the family proves harder to grasp. In Father's words to him, ". . . since Nettie was oldest and a girl, she had to take Mother's place. And whereas Harrison was a grown boy and so strong, he was needed for fieldwork. [Ben] was the youngest and so could be spared" (*Barn*, 9). Like Punch, Ben is so marginalized in this family that they send him away to school. Nettie tells Ben: " 'You were meant to go off and be different. To *be* somebody. Not like us' " (*Barn*, 57). Even though believing it in Ben's best interest, the family focuses on his differences rather than on ways in which he is like them. In fact, Ben's dissimilarity to Nettie and Harrison spares him from the physical labor of farming—yet it earns for him the responsibility of daily care for his father, a charge he initiates, feeling himself unequal to assuming proportional farm duties.

In this care, Ben's distinctions from the family continue to emerge. He brings patience to the job. A belief in his father's being persists in Ben, and he struggles to comprehend it.

... those eyes of his seemed to be looking here, there, everywhere. I don't know why, but all of a sudden I came to think of him as a cave—a deep dark, cave. And there was an animal—of some kind—inside it, inside *him*, hiding ... I had to approach the cave. Had to go into it. (*Barn*, 27)

Ben enters the cave and tries to pull his father out of it. He cares for his father's emotional as well as physical needs. He tells him stories about school, tells him jokes the two had shared privately before, and reads to him. The barn becomes another way to haul Father out of the cave. Whereas Nettie and Harrison admit their father's failing health, Ben distances himself from that knowledge as he fixes hope on Father's inner will to live. Refusing to accept Father's weakening despite his attention, Ben becomes obsessed with the idea of building the barn his father wanted. Ben interprets Father's eye, then hand movements as indications to build. Nettie and Harrison so trust Ben's insight that he convinces them of this necessity. Desperate for his father to get well, Ben strikes a deal. "Leaning over father, [he] shouted, 'We'll promise you the barn if you promise you'll get better' " (*Barn*, 71). "The story shows that the child is father of the man; that dying and building are one cycle; that silence can be eloquent language. Nothing is certain" (Rochman, 40).

Loss of his father threatens Ben's already indefinite sense of identity. His very name, Ben, means "son of." If Ben loses the father, if he remains outsider to his siblings, what and who will he be? On some level, Ben is grateful to his father's illness because it returns him to the family and establishes a role within the family. Building the barn provides him with opportunities to prove his sameness—to himself and to his brother and sister. However, Ben's identity also suffers because of that sickness. His father had allowed Ben to be a child. He provides for Ben when he sends him to school, and he jokes with Ben on the journey. When father and son switch roles as Ben nurses his father, that kind of childhood freedom becomes "a rare lark" (*Barn*, 78). That shift profoundly disturbs Ben and fuses hatred with faithful love of his father.

> It was a cruel thing he had become, and I felt a hatred for it. He
> had abandoned us when we needed him. He has become a child
> when *we* were the children. He had failed us. Oh, I so wanted to
> strike him and make him feel my pain. (*Barn*, 38–39)

Resolving this ambivalence—or perhaps even tolerating that he
can simultaneously despise and love his father—challenges Ben's
identity as his father's son.

The barn grows in significance to Ben and functions as a unifying metaphor in the novel. By acting like adults in building the
barn, Ben hopes to secure his father's existence, his presence in
their lives. And, in ways that Nettie articulates, the barn may be
"just [Ben's] wanting," (*Barn*, 56), not Father's salvation. After
Father's death, before Ben can tell him of the barn's completion,
Ben insists

> "[The barn] was for me—for *me* to give to him. So he would
> thank *me*. Be grateful to *me*. So he'd see I wasn't different."
> (*Barn*, 102)

Here, Ben views the barn as an embodiment of his identity. It
allows him to give something back to his father and to the family;
it accents Ben's sameness. When Schoolmaster Dortmeister
recites the Lord's prayer with Ben before allowing him to go
home, Avi foreshadows not only Father's death but also the barn
as Father's heaven. The family recites the prayer again at
Father's funeral.

> [Ben] said, "When I was reading that 'Our Father,' I wasn't
> thinking of any God. I was thinking of *our* father and wondering
> where he was. And then I thought that if Father is anywhere,
> he's in that barn." (*Barn*, 105)

Throughout the novel, Ben exposes his growing knowledge of
his father's failures. Always "too early or too late" (*Barn*, 102),
Father tinkered with the family's clock, "saying he planned on
finding a way to get time to run backward since, he said, he'd
made a couple of mistakes in his life, but now that he'd practiced

some, he was bound to get things right" (*Barn,* 14). The family moved a number of times, and Father "said the only thing he ever got right was building new houses" (*Barn,* 84). For Ben to build the barn, to get it right, further certifies him as his father's son and as central to the family. The closing chapter of the novel discloses its retrospective posture and cements Ben's identity in this family: " . . . every morning when I get up, the first thing I do is look at the barn. Like father promised: it's something fine to come home to. Still standing. Still strong" (*Barn,* 106).

Beyond the Western Sea: The Escape from Home

The ambiguity of this final chapter leaves Ben's life vague between his 9th and his 79th year. Does he return to school or stay on at the family land? Does he leave home only to return to it? Avi's 1996 novel, *Beyond the Western Sea,* is in two parts. The first bears the title *The Escape from Home,* which introduces another idea about the function of home to the young person. Home stands as a beginning place, but it may also trap an individual and threaten his/her developing identity. As the title to this book suggests, perhaps home is a place to run away from.

The Barn presents Ben as his father's keeper, whereas the phrase "my brother's keeper" consistently occurs in *The Escape from Home.* This simple movement again shifts the integral, sustaining lifelong ties from parents to siblings. Both parents ultimately abandon Maura and Patrick O'Connell. Left by their father in their Irish home of Kilonny, Maura, 15, and Patrick, 12, along with their mother, Annie, must vacate their straw-hut home before they are evicted. It is December of 1850, and the Irish potato famine ravages the country, rendering the poor even more destitute as English landlords reclaim their land from defaulting Irish tenant farmers. Gregory O'Connell (Da) saves the family from the mercy—or lack of mercy—of Lord Kirkle's agent by sending them tickets and money for their emigration to America. Helped by the well-meaning parish priest, they join the river of Irish peasants making their way from Kilonny to Liverpool, where they will board ship for passage to America. Annie O'Connell makes the trip slowly. Her reluctance to depart from her homeland is so palpable that her decision to stay behind seems inevitable. Not only is her son Timothy buried in Ireland, but her persistent coughing also suggests that her death from tuberculosis fast approaches; she recognizes that she is bound to Ireland. Telling Maura and Patrick to board the ship as she walks away, she abandons them. Knowing that now "we are two,"[10] Maura and Patrick draw tight their ties as siblings to survive their perilous journey.

Patrick and Maura create a dynamic team in which readers have faith. In Dickensian fashion, Avi effectively portrays these characters by contrast. Where Patrick acts impetuously, Maura thinks before taking action. Where Maura looks forward and plans for the next step, Patrick lives in the moment. Where Maura suffers injustice quietly, Patrick's deeply held morality commands his voice and action. Despite their differences, the two also share similarities. Familial loyalty and genuine decency mark them. Both trusting, sometimes too trusting, they have faith in the decency of others—a faith that sometimes leads to their disappointment. Charity compels them to reach out to others as needy as they are.

Although quite capable of succeeding alone, Maura soon adds a father figure to their family constellation. Dragged to a temporary shelter by a "runner" taking advantage of Irish immigrants awaiting passage to America, Maura and Patrick meet Horatio Drabble. An actor, stranded and broke in Liverpool, he offers the two protection and practical education about surviving in Mrs. Sonderbye's rooming house. Maura sees in Mr. Drabble someone she can trust at a time when she needs to recuperate and shed responsibility. He willingly steps in to fill that role. Patrick, on the other hand, remains more suspicious of Mr. Drabble. Maura's reliance on Mr. Drabble partly supplants her dependence on Patrick, who feels excluded and resentful.

However, Mr. Drabble's presence does afford Patrick some freedom. With Maura in Mr. Drabble's company, Patrick pursues the runner Toggs, whom he overhears expressing a disquieting interest in Maura. Toggs has already betrayed Patrick by bringing him and his sister to Mrs. Sonderbye's lodging house. Chasing after Toggs promises Patrick atonement for the betrayal and a chance to win Maura back from Mr. Drabble by proving himself a worthy protector.

The relationship between Maura and Mr. Drabble hints in a number of directions. She views him as a father figure and turns over to him many of the onerous details of preparing for the trip. In return, she extends to him the honor of family as she offers him her mother's ticket to America. However, Mr. Drabble's intentions toward Maura are not so clear. Is he an indigent soul who performs Shakespearean monologues on the forsaken Liverpool streets, as he would have others believe, or is he, as Mrs. Sonderbye suggests, a conceited windbag? Is he, as Patrick finds, simply a talkative but empty nuisance? Is he, as Maura believes, a reliable older guide? Or does he have romantic designs on Maura? Although Mr. Drabble's true nature remains unresolved until book two, Avi's physical description of him hints at his ineffectualness.

> He was a long, lanky, bony man—thirty or so, she guessed—with so little flesh upon his bones that when he stood it seemed more an unfolding than a rising. His smile was as wide as his face. His large brown eyes and a thatch of straw-colored hair hanging like a tasseled curtain over his face and ears conspired to create the look of a simple fellow. (*Escape*, 106)

These florid descriptions immediately follow the introduction of a character into the story's plot. They tend toward caricature, the shorthand of stereotype. However, as in Dickens, readers should be wary of accepting the stereotype as totally revelatory. Even these characters carry the potential to deceive. Names, too, indicate personality. Horatio, as Drabble himself informs readers, was Hamlet's friend; in Avi's own fiction, Horatio in *Punch with Judy* proves true and trustworthy; Horatio Alger moves from rags to riches. Yet the surname Drabble, with its dull and ineffective denotation and connotation, seems to contradict the noble attributes of Horatio. One reviewer writes that these "larger-than-life characters [amplified by their rich associations] . . . lend themselves to reader's theater."[11]

Maura and Patrick's emigration functions as one ballast of this plot-intensive novel. "While you actually do have to turn the pages for yourself here, the task soon feels like it's out of your hands as Avi's tense, twisting storytelling takes over. . . . The suspense and the shifting among various points of view are expertly deployed. . . ."[12] Maura and Patrick's story begins the narrative, covering the first 34 pages, the first eight short chapters, of text. Then Avi explores another kind of family, that of the privileged 11-year-old Sir Laurence Kirkle, son of Lord Kirkle, member of the queen's treasury bench and known to readers as the McConnells' inhumane landlord. In many ways, this is the kind of family from whom Charlotte Doyle runs away—the very course of action Laurence himself will take. Avi introduces the family in medias res as Laurence is about to receive a beating from his older brother, Albert, a thrashing orchestrated and overseen by his father. "The Kirkle family motto [is] chiseled below the mantel. Glumly, Laurence reads it now: For Country, Glory—for Family, Honor" (*Escape*, 36). The discordance between family, honor, and the whipping about to take place strikes loudly. Denied the opportunity to defend himself, Laurence pleads both his innocence and for mercy. Sir Kirkle affords his younger son neither; instead, he insists on the obedience due the older son by the younger son. Avi again portrays these siblings in contrast to each other. Where Albert exacts punishment unjustly, Laurence demands fairness. Where Albert holds the powerful position of elder son, Laurence enjoys his father's true favor—a preference unexpressed and therefore misunderstood by his younger son. Where Albert exploits his power, Laurence is rendered powerless.

Avi reveals much about the family after Laurence runs away from it. Although Lord Kirkle genuinely wants the return of his son, he maintains the proprietary distance from the messy situation. Acting partly against his wife's desire to protect the family's reputation from public indiscretion, he hires a private investigator, Mr. Phineas Pickler, to find Laurence. Lord Kirkle withholds the truth about Laurence's beating, a truth that would provide not only a motive for the departure but also a more accurate physical description of the boy, whose torn clothes and scarred cheek identify him. The interview attests to the family's high value on breeding, their wealth, their pomposity, their invest- ment in appearance, and, ultimately, their dishonesty.

Mr. Pickler proves an interesting choice for Lord Kirkle's job. A former policeman, he is somewhat foolishly taken in by the lord's appearance of propriety, which enables him to believe fully in the information Lord Kirkle gives him. Pickler's lack of thorough questioning misleads him. Mr. Pickler's own stable, nuclear fam- ily—a wife who waits up for him to return home and two children who sleep soundly as he gazes upon them—prevents him from being able to entertain the possibility of violence in Lord Kirkle's family.

In a later scene, Albert further adds to this duplicitous family portrait. His violent nature, given rein by his father as Albert beats Laurence, takes shape as he travels into the city of London to hire his own, less honorable, private detective.

> Sir Albert pulled the bell next to a brass plate proclaiming:
>
> Brother's Keepers, Ltd.
> Mr. Matthew Clemspool
> Sole Agent
>
> From deep within he heard a clanging noise.
> Not long after, the front door creaked open. A rather portly man of middle age and height peered out. His smooth face was not unlike a cherub's, round, red, rosy. His head was bald but for a fringe of hair that ran ear to ear at the back, an incomplete halo. He held his plump fingers before him as if plucking—and sounding—the invisible strings of a harp. The cutaway coat he wore was gray, his cravat a fashionable maroon. When he recog- nized his young caller, he blossomed into an agreeable smile.
> (*Escape*, 64)

Like the angelic references throughout this description, "Brother's Keepers" seems an especially ironic appellation here, given that

Albert hires Clemspool to prevent his brother's return. The Kirkle brothers' animosity toward each other stands in direct opposition to the McConnell siblings' affectionate dependence on one another. Throughout this novel Avi creates surrogate families. Maura and Patrick take in Mr. Drabble. Similarly, Clemspool poses as caretaker to Laurence as one way to ensure Laurence's emigration to America; he even announces Laurence as his own son. Finding the tattered, dirty boy on the train, he ingratiates himself to him. Even more than the weary but self-reliant and capable McConnells, Laurence needs and "*likes* being taken care of. He expects it" (*Escape*, 114). The confusion that clouds Laurence's understanding of his place in his family begins to surface in his relationship with Clemspool. However, rather than running away because he does not understand himself or his father's actions, Laurence becomes motivated to flee for the right reasons: He cannot trust Clemspool.

Laurence's troubled home denies him a firm sense of belonging in a family and a constant sense of identity. He does not know the depth of his father's affection for him—nor is he aware of the intensity of his brother's hatred for or his mother's dislike of him. He takes money from his father in order to escape from a home that refuses him a place and then brands himself a criminal, a thief. (Of course, readers know that the real thief is Lord Kirkle, whose rent monies originate with the Irish peasants of Kilonny.) Early in his journey he does not want to be identified as a Kirkle, and so he leaves behind the name of the family that has no place for him. In its stead, he takes the name Worthy. With Dickensian insight, this name poses a formative challenge to Laurence's identity. Near the end of the novel, he articulates the profundity of his identity crisis:

> Clinging to the ladder, Laurence contemplated leaping into the water. Drowning was, he thought, the only way to save himself, his name, his family. "I don't want to be me," he whispered. "I don't. . . . I don't belong to anyone. . . ."
> But he did not want to die.
> From deep within the boy came a sound, half-sigh, half-moan, the sound of something breaking. He began to weep. The

tears began softly but soon became deep racking sobs of bewilderment. "I can't be me anymore," he cried to the darkness. "I can't!"

He knew then that if he were to live, he could no longer be the person he'd been mere days ago. He'd have to become someone else, though who he had no idea. If he could get to America, he thought, perhaps he could be that someone." (*Escape*, 264–65)

Avi's readers will find it just and satisfying that Laurence casts off his old identity and determines to construct a new one while he hides out on board the hulk-remains of *The Seahawk*, the very ship that affirmed Charlotte Doyle's individuality.

Laurence's confession about self goes out to 10-year-old Fred, one of the homeless runners for the Lime Street Association. Sergeant Rumpkin acts as head of this ragtag family organized to bilk arriving immigrants. Fagan-like in disposition, Sergeant Rumpkin nonetheless provides the homeless boys in his association with the very sense of purpose and belonging absent from Laurence's life. Within this surrogate family, Toggs and Fred vie for the favor of Sergeant Rumpkin. Initially, their rivalry takes the form of an active business competition to see who can bring home to Sergeant Rumpkin the most money. However, in a scene reminiscent of that between Lord Kirkle and his two sons, Sergeant Rumpkin chooses to believe the older Toggs over the faithful Fred; he mistakenly trusts that Fred's loyalty will enable him to suffer this rejection. The ousted son, marginalized like Laurence, turns against the family. In helping Laurence to escape the clutches of Clemspool and the claws of Pickler, both of whom have enlisted, at prime rates, the assistance of the Lime Street Runners' Association, Fred accepts not belonging to anyone but himself. As he and Laurence share family histories, as he devotes time and energy to protect and assist Laurence, he behaves like a true brother.

Avi explores ways in which bonds between friends and among family members can ignore the high borders of class lines. Wealthy, unsure runaway Laurence eventually crosses paths with poor, confident emigrant Patrick. They meet on the dock where

Toggs has coerced Laurence into stealing money from a moored boat. As the police appear, Toggs runs, leaving Laurence to fend for himself. Luckily, Patrick, out looking for Toggs, finds Laurence instead and helps him. "As in Dickens' works, coincidence [like this] is not just a plot surprise but a revelation that those who appear to be far apart—the powerful and the 'failures'—are, in fact, intimately connected" (Rochman, 930). In Laurence, Patrick sees someone more privileged than he is but someone whom he assesses as worse off than he. First he asks Laurence for his name and gives his name in return. They then exchange stories, and Patrick inquires about Laurence's family.

> "Have you no family with you?" he ventured.
> Laurence shook his head.
> "Traveling alone then?"
> "Yes."
> "Sure, you've got it much harder than me," Patrick said. "I have Maura." (*Escape*, 163)

For Patrick, family serves as identifier and unifier. Patrick and Laurence spend the night on board the ship *Charity*, a floating church run by Reverend Bartholomew. Despite the differences in their classes, their families, and their religions, they find true friendship and brotherhood with one another, a fraternity mocked by the ship's motto, "Am I my brother's keeper?" As a result of true concern, Patrick extends to Laurence a place in his family by offering to Laurence Annie O'Connell's ticket to America. Even though Patrick cannot make good on this promise to Laurence because he first honors Maura's giving the ticket to Mr. Drabble, he vows to help Laurence stow away on the *Robert Peel* to America—and Laurence trusts Patrick to do so. In this sense, Patrick becomes his "brother's" keeper.

Beyond the Western Sea, Book One: The Escape from Home incorporates the variety of family constellations appearing throughout Avi's fiction. Although difficult to draw convincing conclusions about a work awaiting its complementary volume, this novel pulls again at threads of family. The strong evocation of a downtrodden, famine-ridden Ireland and emigrant-crowded,

"Liverpool dockside slums, with the desperate pressed together in a foul, teeming hell" (Rochman 1996, 930) establish a social and economic background that demands escaping from home. To the extent that location defines self, these cities cannot nurture a hopeful spirit, an independent, successful sense of self. They will give birth only to self-serving gluttons like Sergeant Rumpkin or wandering, wondering boys like Toggs. Because their wealth depends on the exploitation of others, more privileged individuals such as Laurence or Lord Kirkle can derive only a fractured sense of self. To be whole, they must leave home.

Yet, even as Maura, Patrick, and Laurence escape from this home, they move toward another. They have reinforced and extended to others the bonds of family, and, to a certain extent, they take that family with them. Maura and Patrick escape the poverty of their home in order to join with their father to recreate a new kind of family. To truly find himself, Laurence escapes from the family that permits him no identity. Avi charges his readers with the tremendously powerful knowledge that family forms self, yet self must sometimes escape from home in order to survive. He complicates that insight by adding that family also travels with one and may never be wholly eluded. Perhaps *Book Two: Lord Kirkle's Money* will continue to consider the complex intertwining of self, family, and home.

9. Avi as Writer

A gentle, but adversarial relationship.

—Richard Jackson[1]

The following discussion is an edited version of a conversation between Avi and Richard Jackson that took place at Simmons College summer institute titled "A Room of One's Own" on 26 July 1995.

Avi: Thomas Mann, the great German writer, once said that the difference between the professional writer and people who write is that for the professional writer, the writing is harder. And that's exactly the opposite of what most people think. I visit kids in schools, and they assume that I became a writer because I had it easy, because I got As in school and so forth. Not me. I flunked out of one high school. I required tutoring in school. Yes, there are natural writers, but I'm not one of them. Writing can be torturous. Sometimes it flows, but usually it is extremely difficult. One can think of writing in a very different way than in the way most nonwriters think about it. A good novel, for the reader, has a logical construction. In fiction, one writes 200, 300, 400, even 900 pages of sustained logic. That's difficult because people are not inherently logical. Logic imposes a structure. What artistry is all about, what creativity does is to experience chaos (which pervades the universe) and shape it into some sort of cohesive rational structure so that the chaos becomes comprehensible. Creating art is the desperate attempt to try to make that which is irrational, rational. To make some sense out of existence.

149

Through this conversation, we will share how Dick and I work together. There are a couple of things that you have to know at the beginning. I was born with dysgraphia, which means I have problems writing. It has plagued me all my life. Dick, on the other hand, is dyslexic. So I have trouble writing, and he has trouble reading; that seems to be at the core of our working relationship!

I believe that the story is mine, but the published book is a collaborative effort. My hand holds the pencil; Dick sharpens it. When I work with a good editor, I leave energized and excited. I leave thinking, "At last, I understand the book, what it's all about."

With but one exception, in the books on which we have worked together, I present the idea to Dick. The one exception: I was visiting Dick and his wife and we were in a restored 1930s theater in Stanford. We were watching an old movie, and at one point he leaned over and said to me, "Some day I'd like to see you write a book with just dialogue. I'll give you a few 'he said' and 'she saids.' " Now, I don't know why Dick said that. I don't know if it was a joke or not, but it got to me. Out of that comment came the book, *"Who Was That Masked Man, Anyway?"* But that's the only time he gave me an idea for a book.

I talk to Dick about a variety of particular projects. Sometimes he has the manuscript, and he responds to it. But at other times, when I'm halfway through writing something and I'm having a problem, we'll communicate.

I usually begin with a combination or a situation and a character. In fact, I try to keep away from the ending as long as I can. I'll even stall as I approach it. Literally, I begin on page 1. Usually, I work on the first chapter over and over and over again until I get the kind of tonalities in the voices that I find comfortable and which feel correct. Then I go on to the second chapter. But even as I do that, I go back to the first one. And I rewrite the book at this stage maybe 40 or 50 times. Over and over again. I have only the vaguest sense of what I'm doing, and I certainly do not have an ending in mind.

I joke to myself that I write very slowly quickly. That describes this endless revision. Partly, it has to do with dysgraphia. But this

A4

Chapter 35

Brian and Lawrence Make Plans

Change Admiral to Nelson *317*

Duke of Wellington

On the <u>Charity</u>, the Reverend Gideon Bartholomew concluded the service. ~~Carefully,~~ he removed his surplice and turned to face the chairs, Only ~~then did he~~ realize *that* Fred had gone. ~~For a moment the minister paused to~~ ~~speculate upon whether~~ the boy would, as promised, deliver his letter to the police office. ~~Inwardly, he~~ sighed, telling himself that sometimes he was too trusting. ~~Perhaps~~ ~~he should not~~ have given *him* the penny ~~before~~ the task was completed. Now he had no way ~~of knowing~~ if the letter ~~had~~ *would* reach*ed* its destination. ~~He would have to go himself.~~ All he said, however, as he came cheerfully down the aisle toward Brian and Lawrence, was, "I see our other friend has *left*. ~~Glad~~ *That* I'm pleased you boys remained, I trust the words of the Lord were a comfort."

"Please, your honor," ~~Brian~~ *he* said, "Last night you said you'd take me back to where my sister is, to the lodging house run by that Mrs. Sonderbye's."

"And so I did," Mr. Bartholomew replied. He was trying to think how he might hold the boys a while so as to give the police a chance to respond just in case the letter was

All during the service Brian had closed his eyes and said his prayers lest the Protestant service harm him. Now he looked up.

During 1995, Avi used this page from the manuscript-in-progress of his *Beyond the Western Sea.*

example is typical of a page of my work as I'm writing and am involved in the process I've just described. (See illustration on page 151.) I work on the computer and then will go over the computer copy many, many times. Then I'll print it out and go over the hard copy. Then I insert the changes from the printed text back into the computer and start all over again.

I believe deeply that the hardest part of writing is reading. One simply cannot be a writer unless he learns to read well. One writes and is called a writer, but one has to be able to read what's been written *as* a reader. It is the response as reader that enables the writer to make the necessary adjustments and changes to the story. For me it's a totally intuitive process.

Some of the things I do: I take notes. I will write and describe the character in the text and then separate these out, put them on a separate sheet of paper and develop character sketches. I don't do them as a prefatory step to writing. Then I keep these by my side while I write about that character. Occasionally I will glance at the character sketch as a way of reminding myself.

My early writing as a playwright continues to influence the way I conceptualize a story and its structure. The only courses in writing I took were in playwrighting, not fiction writing. My understanding of the way a plot moves forward derives from my sense of and experience in the theater. I change these outlines all the time. They get revised; they are not complete. I consider them maps that enable me to move forward from one spot to the next. At the same time, though, I need to know very carefully the place about which I am writing. What does the ship on which [Charlotte Doyle] traveled look like? I visited many ships as I did research for that book.

People often ask me how long it takes me to write a book. I wrote the first draft of *S.O.R. Losers* in one day. On the other hand, I worked on *Bright Shadow* for 14 years before it was published. So there's an enormous range which has to do with a clarity of vision. I'm not always clear. Sometimes it takes longer. I can't read the book well enough to understand how it works or doesn't work.

When I finish a draft of a book, I usually, but not always, share the book with Dick. It's important for you to know that he has not accepted all my books. Nor should he. Some of the books that he has rejected, let me hasten to say, either have not been published at all because he has convinced me that they were not good and his judgment matched that of others. But other books that he has turned down have gone on to publication elsewhere.

Richard: You should know that I live in California, work out of a bedroom in my house, and have a lovely view of the mountains from my windows. This is an extremely good life for an editor because I work in my head just as writers work in theirs. I don't go to publishing meetings. I file most of the pressing work on the floor, at my feet. My wife is understanding.

I read manuscripts aloud to myself and sometimes to others, too. If I get a picture-book text and decide I must make an offer, I always retype the manuscript first. I want to get the text in my fingers. I have no idea why this tells me something, but it does. I pick up word repetitions which may be right or may not be right—and which otherwise I might miss. I learn through my fingers—who knows why?

The trick for any editor is to keep many books and many characters straight, not to veer unconsciously into using a character's name from another writer's book. Now, as several writers who know me well can attest, I don't always succeed in doing this—perhaps it's the floor filing system. However, I know I must bring a powerful concentration to my work with a writer, to our work together. Also, I must bring my ignorance; this is very useful to a writer. If I don't understand or have missed something in the book, it is fairly safe to presume that the child reader might not understand either.

There may be, in any one day, 20 books, picture books and novels, that come up for discussion. Not all of them are Avi's! Only one or maybe two at a time are his; he is now working on a two-volume book of approximately 900 manuscript pages. That has taken our attention for some time.

ORCHARD BOOKS

January 26, 1995

Sir!

Here's the first part of the letter. Nothing wholesale till page 71 of the version I have here (Chapter 7, toward the end).

I wonder if Laurence would--rather easily, it seems--call his father a coward. That's a pretty cheeky accusation; and I don't get the feeling that, though they're reportedly pals, young Laurence is so very much at ease with his father--or would be in 1851. Also, the idea of cowardice is perhaps beyond Laurence's rather young 12? He might feel it in himself, but would he charge his father with it?

On page 89 (toward end of Chapter 10), I'm surprised at the apparent quantity of bills still left in Laurence's hand after the thief has run off. Can it be clearer there?

Page 102 (middle Chapter 12): "Snips" crops up for Stokes. More interesting is my concern about how Lady Kirkle "sweeps" out of the room. I can't read in this what she feels about being dismissed. She seems meeker than "sweeps."

Page 104: Not positive, but I believe this is the only space break I've come upon so far. Could this break be the start of a short new chapter instead? We do have a couple of short ones coming up....

Page 106: The final paragraphs here end and end again; it's clear at top of page that once he's focused on Euston Station he'll be heading there. [We have discussed Stokes on the phone. I feel there's too much thinking things through with him--or we see too much of him working toward decisions. When he's on stage, at least in these plotting sections, my attention flags. I want, as a kid reader, to be focused on the kids. When they aren't there, I fidget.]

Page 110 (near beginning of Chapter 10): I don't quite get the Will business and how Mr. Clemspool expects to benefit (same on page 111). Is Mr. C. also in the employ of Lord Kirkle and therefore aware of the contents of the Will?

95 Madison Avenue · New York. New York 10016 · (212) 686-7070 · Fax (212) 213-6435

Letter from editor Richard Jackson about *Beyond the Western Sea;* used by permission, Avi.

Avi: Like most writers, I am also a reader. I've always enjoyed the Victorian novel. I read many of them and enjoy them greatly. I noticed a discrepancy in my visits to schools: On one hand, we're told that kids are reading shorter and shorter books, but if one asks the young people what they read outside of school assignments,

ORCHARD BOOKS

Page 122 (Chapter 14 middle): I think Laurence's first sight of the station goes on too long; not sure why exactly, but I got impatient....

Page 128 (Chapter 15): Not sure why I think of this just now, but you use "Mr." throughout. I wonder, looking into Dickens, if he doesn't make a distinction about when to use it and when not. Are negative characters called simply by their last names in order that their darkness be acknowledged (Mr. being cozier)? The consistent use of "Mr." implies a young narrator's point of view perhaps, in which all adults are Mr. or Mrs. or Miss; is that best?

Chapter 16 we referred to on the phone, and I have above re: page 106. I think wherever a kid character is not at hand, things get long, seem to drag a bit; particularly with Mr. Stokes. Anything you can speed him up along here? 'Twould help.

Page 146 (two pages into Chapter 19): I'm surprised at the reference to "rigging"; how does that figure on a side-wheeler?

Page 153, Toggs heading deeper into the city. Somehow the description here doesn't work for me because he's seen it all before and wouldn't describe it as the words do. Maybe trim....

Page 173 (Chapter 22 middle): I wonder that Laurence doesn't react with startlement when Mr. Clemnspool grips his arm as they step from the carriage. Wouldn't he note that as odd, surprising, suddenly sinister???

That's it for this moment. I've been distracted away, probably for the rest of the day.

'Bye,

95 Madison Avenue · New York, New York 10016 · (212) 686-7070 · Fax (212) 213-6435

Letter from editor Richard Jackson about *Beyond the Western Sea;* used by permission, Avi.

they report reading long books. For example, if one asks a class of fifth graders how many of them have read a Stephen King novel or a Michael Crichton novel, half of the kids raise their hands. In short, young readers are more than capable, if they choose to be and if they are engaged enough, of reading long books.

I decided I would write a long book that deals with an individual moment in world and American history; I would deal with religion and I would deal with politics. *Beyond the Western Sea* is quite the most difficult thing that I have ever done. Sometimes it is fun, but most days it is difficult to maintain the concentration. Every once in a while Dick or I will say, as he said to me yesterday, "Are you aware that Dickens started to write . . .

Richard: *Nicholas Nickleby* in February of 1838. It was published in October of the same year. That's a lot of handwriting.

Avi: I have learned much about Victorian novels in this process, about what these writers accomplished and how they did so. Trollope and Dickens were extraordinary, remarkable.

In the case of this two-volume book, which starts with *The Escape from Home*, I had completed a draft of the first volume. I thought that if it didn't work with Dick, it won't work anywhere else. Dick has always allowed me to take risks. Dick looked at it and probably ran to his banker and said, "Can we afford to do this in one way or another?" We created a system of working together on this manuscript which differs somewhat from our past projects. The last book we did together, *The Barn*, had 65 manuscript pages. This was more than 10 times that amount. *The Barn* I submitted as complete; this one didn't even come close.

The essence of our process is talk, talk, talk. Dick intervenes in a variety of ways, everything from "I think chapter 6 should come after chapter 95" or "this part is dull and just doesn't work" or "there's not enough excitement" or something like that. It can be as simple as picking up a single word I dropped to calling for a substantial revision.

I love to revise. There's nothing I love more than Dick calling me and saying "I think there's a problem." I show off by solving the problem on the telephone, sitting down, rewriting that part, and faxing it to him within an hour.

Richard: And then I show off by responding to the fax within five minutes!

236

Holding up the bottle.

"Medicine," Lawrence returned.

"Fair likely." He pulled the cork and sniffed it.

"Some fancy drink, you stole."

"It is medicine," Lawrence insisted.

"Never mind," Mr. Davis said, ~and~ shoveling *and* the food ~as well~

~as the drink~ into one of his pockets. "I ~have~ *got* a job ~that~

I ~need~ you ~to~ *can* help me with."
what do you mean, Job?

"~For money?~" Lawrence asked, ~thinking Mr. Davis was~

~about to employ him.~

"~Of course it's about money. What else is there?~"

"~But . . .~ "

·Mr. Davis reached out ~and~ took hold of Lawrence's

shoulder and squeezed it painfully. "I don't want ~any~

objections," he snapped. "Mind, if I wanted to I could

pitch you into the water quick as a wink. Do you know

when they would find you? Next week, maybe. ~So let's~
All ~Right then, let's~
~understand ourselves,~ You're going to do what I tell you

to do. Do you understand me?"
I've found a way to get some

Lawrence, thoroughly frightened, nodded.

"All right then, ~what's your name?~" he demanded.

"Lawrence."

"Lawrence it is. Here's the pitch. Down the way,

there's a pretty coastal trader easy on her moorings. All

fancied up she is, with the sniff of money fairly oozing

out of her. I watched as she came in and I saw her crew--

Awrence shook his head

Do you understand-

"Yes, sir"

Lawrence moaned. He was forgotten.

I'm in need of money

During the summer of 1995, Avi used examples from *Beyond the Western Sea.*

Avi: He sends me back the manuscript with all these marks in it. I look through it very casually and enter most of them into my text. Then I throw out the old manuscript, and I rewrite it from the revised one. I no longer know what's his and what's mine. I just respond to the new manuscript all over again. Then he gets it again, and we go back and forth in this way. It's highly collaborative.

Sometimes I'll call him up and say, "I've been thinking, I'm going to change this whole character in a totally different way." We talk about that idea and I return to the manuscript to make changes. Or he calls me and says, "There are two boys in this book, yet they seem somewhat similar. Can we alter that?" I do, then the book changes radically. So it goes until the book is done.

When the book is done (when we both think it's done), I know that in a week or so I'll get a call that begins, "I've been thinking. . . ." For example, when *The True Confessions of Charlotte Doyle* was done, Dick called me up. "I've been thinking," he says, "Charlotte never says good-bye to the crew." He was right—he found a glitch in the story. He didn't tell me what to do, just pointed out the problem. I sat down to write this last part of the "finished" book, though it's not the novel's ending. As Charlotte says good-bye to each of the crew members, I'm crying because I'm saying good-bye to Charlotte, too. It's my favorite part of the book. I finished that part, sent it off, and never adjusted it again. That's the way it works. It's that simple; it's that complex.

Some books are very hard to write. Some easy. I don't understand why. *Nothing but the Truth* was so easy to write it unnerved me. Halfway through it I thought I was crazy because it seemed to be working so well. I handed the manuscript to Dick, and he simply said, "Keep going." That's all I needed. Some books see a lot of intervention; some do not.

Richard: I love the word "intervention." I've never thought of the process, but then I'm on the giving end. I'm essentially a very private, shy person and don't meet people well at parties. Yet I think about them, observe them at a distance. It's the same way with people in books. Two weeks after I've read a manuscript—in the middle of the night—I'll wake up thinking, "Wait a second, there's something I don't understand, or there's something psychologically missing." That's when I get on the blower. Art hangs around in one's head, not always immediately self-revealing.

If indeed my work were simply going to the banker and asking whether we can afford to publish this or that book, I wouldn't be here today. I might be wearing a suit more often than I do, but I sure as hell wouldn't be an artist or an editor. And I do think editors are artists, of artistic temperament. Not necessarily creative but interpretive. We are not failed writers, just people who can see patterns and textures, who can hear a variety of sounds at one time.

I wanted to read to you a letter I received from a librarian a couple of weeks ago, a letter of sympathy because one of my favorite writers, Frances Temple, died earlier this month. The librarian's condolence articulates the essence of editorial work.

"I once saw a bell ringer in a very old church in England on film. There were several bells in the tower, and he moved deftly from one to the other, pulling mightily on each in turn until his feet swung off the floor. The trick, of course, was to move swiftly enough to keep the bells all ringing more or less simultaneously, yet in order.

"Metaphorically speaking, you are like a bell ringer. And each of your authors [is] like a bell. The voice is in the bell, but it takes the bell ringer to free it—and to keep the bells pealing. For a long time after the ringer stops pulling the ropes, the sound can be heard and literally felt hanging in the air.

"Frances Temple's voice was like the ringing of a bell in the air. The greatest resonance and clarity. And it is still heard and felt. Thank you for that."

Now, that is why I am an editor. Not to get letters like this, but to matter that much to people whose work matters that much in the world.

[In his *Horn Book* article "We," Richard Jackson further illuminates his ideas about the working relationship between writer and editor.]

"Writing is an act of generosity, of showing readers unlit corners of character, the contents of a closet, the color of a sky— none of it crucial to a plot, perhaps, but all of it contributing. Very often what's generous in a book has come out during the process of revision, from first draft to second, from fourth draft to fifth. Judy Blume loves revising because she learns more of what she knew already but hadn't written down.

Revising requires us to think further. And for each book the process is different. Avi's *The True Confessions of Charlotte Doyle* was edited line for line, very closely, because the voice had to be just right. He and I exchanged chapters by express mail: he'd be revising one clump while I'd be fiddling, often reading the text aloud to myself, on the next. We had the best fun, and he continually surprised me with new thinking.

In *Nothing but the Truth*—a very different book—form, not language, was the talking point. There was not the issue of sustaining a single voice—the whole point was to have lots of voices; indeed, some of the language for the school-board candidate is intentionally gobbledygook. The kid at the center of the novel is no writer, so Avi wasn't going after beautiful prose. Instead, his idea from the beginning was a story of irony in which the reader determines the meaning of many disparate pieces. As a novelist, Avi is always interested in another way to tell a story. And there often *is* another way—one that editors sometimes can see more clearly than writers themselves. That's where editors are useful: as sounding boards. The writer does "sit down alone and do it" but needn't *feel* he or she is alone."[2]

Avi: One must understand how important Dick is to so many people. He's worked with and developed significant writers for children and young adults like Judy Blume, Gary Paulsen, Paula Fox, and Cynthia Rylant, to name just a few. One can't look at the landscape of children's literature in the last generation without seeing Dick's creativity in it. All of us who work with him adore him, and we love to swap stories about him. I've heard lots of stories about editors, and some of them can be very nasty, believe me. Editors can be cruel and hard on writers. Yet, I have never, ever heard negative stories about Dick. Ever. He may even have deserved them, but still I don't hear them.

He may talk about having 20 books on his desk or on his floor each day, but I still can call him up and quite rudely say, "Look, in chapter 16, that third paragraph . . ." and he's there instantly. I

44

~~was put greatly~~ *instart* at my ease. *my heart truly melted* I *could have*
shead tears of
gratitude
"Ah," he said with the greatest refinement,

"It is Miss Doyle, our young lady passenger." He

~~even~~ lifted his hat in a salute. "Captain Jaggery

at your service," he said.

I took a wobbly step in his direction. My

sense of neausa was intense but ~~I may have even~~
—I— *in my best modest, simpery*
tried to curtsey. "Please, sir," I whispered, my *Big eyed way.*

eyes, ~~no doubt~~, imploring, "I shouldn't be here. I

must go
~~need to be~~ back ~~to~~ Liverpool."

When he did not reply I looked up. The kindness I had seen when he had greeted me was gone.
Now he was looking at me with cold and hostile
eyes, showing such severity that I was taken aback
and momentarily frightened. But then, the very next
moment, that look passed. He seemed to have a change
of mind or heart. He smiled ~~again~~ brilliantly,

warmly. He even laughed, a robust, manly laugh.
Miss Doyle
"Return to Liverpool?" he said. "~~It's out of~~
I'm afraid it's
~~the question, Miss Doyle.~~ ~~It's~~ my obligation to
of the maritime trade.
inform you of this cardinal principal there is no

place on earth where, ~~so to speak~~, time is money,

as it is on board a ship. We are well off and we

shall continue off and on. God willing, we shall

touch no land but welcome ports.
I can see you
— both deserve as
Such Rude   *you used to*
"I am sorry you ~~do not~~ have ~~better~~ company. I *Betty.*

Manuscript page from *True Confessions of Charlotte Doyle;* copyright
Avi.

don't know how he does that. It's deeply impressive. I've come to
presume that I can rely on him in this immediate, responsive way.
It is rare for me to say, "Can I trouble you? Are you working on
one of Janet's books or one of Rachel's or one of Brian's? I'll get
off the telephone if you are." I simply say, "Here I am. Help me."

And he is always, always there. That quality is rare in my life, and it's something to cherish.

One of the unique aspects of children's books is that all of us who work in it create books together. At Orchard Books, I work so closely with Maggie Herold, who is in charge of all copyediting, she's become a friend of mine. Or I talk to the president of the company, Neal Porter, or with Skye Stewart in marketing. I think of all these people as my friends. All of us are engaged in the making of the books together. We are collaborators.

10. Avi as Subject

> Most fiction is shaped by geography and permeated by autobiography, even when it is not trying to be.
>
> Ross MacDonald[1]

Avi reports that a young adult said about reading his books, "When you get to the end of them, you have to keep thinking about them."[2] Although Avi confesses that he was complimented, he quickly adds that he did not think his young reader meant it that way. Avi interpreted her tone as annoyance at having to do more than simply put a book down and as quickly forget about it. Not every one of Avi's readers reacts with the enthusiasm of the young reader who wrote to him declaring that she had read *The True Confessions of Charlotte Doyle* 16 times. "It's all I want to talk about. It's all I want to read, and now my mother says I'm not allowed to talk about it."[3] She begged him to write a sequel, if not for herself, then for her mother, who had heard enough about Charlotte. Both these anecdotes provide compelling reasons that teachers are drawn to using Avi's books in the classroom: Young readers like them, and they *think* about them. Avi's books offer a substantive alternative to the mindless books many students read—and forget—on their own as well as providing relief to the classics that have so long been a part of required reading lists. Avi's titles, most notably *The Fighting Ground, The True Confessions of Charlotte Doyle,* and *Nothing but the Truth* now appear as a regular, refreshing part of the school curriculum, joining the work of other young adult writers such as Robert Cormier, Walter Dean Myers, and Cynthia Voigt. Like Avi, these writers have gained acceptance largely through their popularity with kids and their critical approbation from adults.

School Visits

Avi has made a commitment to his audience, evidenced in his frequent appearances in schools throughout the country. During these visits he stands apart from many of his colleagues by making real demands on his constituency. Because all authors wish to greet a knowledgeable forum, Avi has evolved a set of guidelines in anticipation of his visit to a school to ensure maximum investment and return for students. In 1991, he copyrighted this material in a 20-page booklet, "Making the Most of a School Visit: Ideas, Suggestions, Hopes."[4] Avi addresses teachers about these directions. He points to his experience that "the greater degree of contact your kids have with my books—the more successful the visit will be" ("Visit," 1). Avi agrees with the Southern California Children's Bookseller Association's advice that "the success of your event will *absolutely* depend on your students' familiarity with your guest's books" ("Visit," 1). Avi frowns on either book talks or last-minute readings of his books as substitutes for the students' actual engagement with the book itself.

Because he wants student involvement, Avi insists that sessions of less than 45 minutes do not allow for students "to relax, size me up, learn to trust me, so that they may respond with the questions that are important to them" ("Visit," 4). Avi begins many of his talks with an intimate sharing of his own beginnings as a writer. He does not go back to his earliest writing as a boy of eight or nine, when he was creating scripts from his own imagination. From the beginning, Avi's attempts at writing revealed his difficulty with the printed word. Avi was diagnosed as suffering from dysgraphia, "an impairment of the ability to write, usually caused by brain dysfunction or disease."[5]

Because Avi wants to engage fully with all students, he often requests having an audience of kids with learning disabilities. He knows how discouraging it can be to work as hard as possible and still not measure up to parental, school, or societal expectations.

During a school visit Avi magnifies his early writing attempts. He uses an overhead projector to show students his own high school English papers heavily marked with the teacher's corrections in red pencil. Although these papers hardly encouraged the adolescent Avi in his determination to be a writer, they often do not look unlike the markings of his own editor on current manuscripts. The sharing of his first "manuscripts" signals Avi's intent to be honest with young people, to remind them that he was once a student himself—and not a very successful one. The juxtaposition between his initial writings for classroom assignments and his later professional writings powerfully suggest how much the procedure of writing remains one of constant hard work and correction, of revision and rewriting. Avi repeatedly talks about his commitment to writing as process. He speaks of himself as "a very slow writer who works quickly" ("Writing," 20). Typically Avi's final manuscript bears little relation to his first drafts, which he confesses he would not reveal to his own cat. He communicates with students that even late versions need rewriting. Typically Avi may go through 40 or 50 "rewrites" seeking the best telling of a story. With excitement mixed with some degree of frustration as well, he describes his process as "endlessly, endlessly rewriting."[6] His friend and fellow writer, Natalie Babbitt, speaks of the great pleasure Avi derives from the process of writing. "I don't think he finds that process easier than the rest of us, but of all the colleagues I know well enough to talk about, he seems to be the most enamoured of simply sitting down and digging into it."[7]

During a school visit students also hear about Avi's love of research and how his own investigative work generates as well as validates his stories. The kids come expecting to listen, and then they ask questions. Having done his homework about the school and the community, Avi might begin a session asking the kids a series of questions about their school, its name, its history. "Who is the school named after? Why is it named after that person? Did everyone agree that it should be named after that person, or was there some conflict? Two hundred years ago, what was happening where the school now stands?" (Markham, 82). Hidden in the answers, Avi asserts, exists all the excitement of learning a part of history and plenty of stories.

Avi seems to think in stories and to see stories everywhere. Recently, just after he moved into his Boulder home, he woke up to a racket on the first floor. Thinking it sounded as if someone had broken in, he went to look and found the kitchen in a mess. He heard sounds in the bathroom and traced the path of the mess there, where he found two raccoons. One was settled in the old claw bathtub, the other hiding underneath it. Avi chased the animals out. As he recounted this story, Avi quickly followed it by saying, "I believe there's a story in there."

Perhaps this ability to create extraordinary stories out of the ordinary parts of daily life partly accounts for Avi's devoted readership. He is one of those authors kids get hooked on. Frequently librarians and teachers work with readers who return their first Avi title with a comment like "Do you have any more books like this one?" "Did Avi write anything else?" "Where can I find a book with a character like Charlotte? or Andy? or Jonathan? or Philip?" What a pleasure to direct such a reader to some 30 other titles that, although different, offer the comfort and familiarity of an author whose one book they responded to positively and energetically.

Teaching Avi's Works

Avi has become an author whose writing generates thoughtful assignments ranging from reading journal responses to whole units exploring in-depth examination of his books, delving into "the deep fabric of the text itself and its creative process" ("Writing," 18). Twice in *Book Links*, a publication of the American Library Association designed for teachers, the editors have turned to an Avi title as the focus for a thematic study of literature. In its comprehensive investigation of a single book rich with possibilities for classroom use, *Book Links* shows teachers effective ways to use *The True Confessions of Charlotte Doyle*.[8] This issue offers teachers suggestions on "Setting the Mood" by turning to other arts, including music, art, and drama. Each page of the guide features a boxed discussion point. The initial one quotes Avi's provocative opening sentence, challenging students to "find other quotes that are significant to the unfolding of the story, identifying why they are important" (*Book Links*, 1226). This teacher's manual concludes with an annotated bibliography of titles, grouped around common themes (voyages of discovery, voyages of disaster, voyages in novels, ships, sails, and shipbuilding) that have the potential to extend involvement with *The True Confessions of Charlotte Doyle* (*Book Links*, 1226–1230). In a later issue, *Book Links* uses a similar format to guide teachers in their use of *Nothing but the Truth*.[9]

Teachers in middle school, high school, and even in graduate school find their own creative ways to present Avi's books with innovative, challenging assignments. For example, students in a Brookline, Massachusetts, middle school reading group are encouraged to keep a reading response journal. In the journal they both react to what they read as well as predict what might yet happen. In addition, the students must concentrate on what questions they want answered as they continue to read the story. Avi—the storyteller, the magician, the truthteller, the risk taker, the subverter—would applaud these journals focused largely on students' unanswered questions.

In one Wellesley, Massachusetts, middle school, the culminating activity for the students, all of whom have read at least six Avi titles, concerns their response to the question "Who is Avi?" For their paper, students must explain the common themes, characters, settings, and plots found in Avi's books, using examples from the many books they have read to support their opinion.

The Writer's Life

These students are too knowledgeably involved with Avi's work to ask the obvious, uninformed question: "Where do your ideas come from?"—a question Avi hears too often and one that he eschews. Still, like Holden Caulfield, these students so admire the writer that they also possess a natural curiosity about the writer's life.

Regular jogging has become part of Avi's writing process. At various points in his life, Avi started, then stopped, then started running again. When he lived in New Hope, Pennsylvania, he ran on a path along a canal. In Boulder, Colorado, his current home, Avi runs the same three-and-one-half mile course each day at midday. Living at the foot of the "Flat Irons" mountains, he runs straight up the slopes to a canyon. Were he to run five miles, he would be able to run into the canyon.

Avi uses his time running as an important part of his work routine. He finds running meditative, a time when he can consider his writing, a time to solve "countless plot problems." Like the laptop computer that travels with him, running is a highly transportable activity. It requires only appropriate shoes and easily carried clothing. Therefore, Avi can take this sport on the road with him as he embarks on an ambitious schedule of school visits and other opportunities to meet with his audience of committed readers.

Always eager for new exploration, Avi has lived in many geographic parts of the country, except in the South. He has lived on the West coast—in San Francisco for a year after he completed an undergraduate degree in history and theater—and for a year in Madison, where he did graduate work in playwrighting at the University of Wisconsin. He returned to his hometown of New York in 1961 to be near the renowned theatrical district of Broadway.

While in New York writing, Avi found full-time employment when he took a job at the New York Public Library as a clerk in the theater collection. Avi enrolled at Columbia University's graduate degree program in library science in part because the theater collection was scheduled to move to Lincoln Center and Avi believed that it would be staffed by those with master's degrees in library science. Another motivation for pursuing a full-time position was his marriage in 1963 to Joan Gainer, a dance coach at the Young Men's Hebrew Association in the Bronx where Avi was a drama coach (Markham, 55).

Avi's degree in library science allowed him to participate in a professional exchange: He assumed the responsibilities of a librarian in England as that librarian took over his position in New York for a year. Avi's first son, Shaun, was two years old at the start of this exchange, and his second son Kevin was born in Great Britain.

Upon their return to the States, Avi settled his family in New Jersey as he took a position as an academic librarian at Trenton State College. The family moved to New Hope, Pennsylvania, just across the state border and the Delaware River from Trenton, into a larger house while Avi worked at Trenton State (Markham, 62). Avi held this position for 17 years, years during which he also taught courses in children's literature at the college, when he began collecting children's books, and, perhaps most importantly, when his children became the first audience for his storytelling.

In 1982, Avi and Joan separated and then divorced. He applied for a position at a library in Connecticut, yet moved instead to Providence, Rhode Island, in 1983 with his second wife, Coppelia Kahn, who had been offered a teaching position at Brown University. During one sabbatical Avi spent time in Oregon. He left Providence for Boulder, Colorado, in late 1995 after a separation from Coppelia.

Clearly, Avi's physical location influences his fiction. His family spent summers on Shelter Island, off the coast of Long Island, New York—a place that inspired *A Place Called Ugly* even as New York sets *Sometimes I Think I Hear My Name*. His earlier historical fiction takes on the settings of Trenton, New Jersey, and then New Hope, Pennsylvania. Later books adopt Providence, Rhode Island, as their location. The jacket of *Something Upstairs* even includes a photograph of Avi standing in front of his home at 15 Sheldon Street in Providence. In fact, "The Providence Preservation Society uses Avi's books as part of its guided [history] tours. . . . In the spring and the fall, tour buses [would] regularly pull into the narrow street in front of Avi's historic house and drop off hundreds of students for a first hand look at the [novel's] setting. Sometimes, if Avi sees a group tour outside his house, he goes out and chats with the students about writing" (Markham, 115–6). He sets *The Barn* in Oregon and has begun to use Boulder as a backdrop.

Avi has already immersed himself in Boulder as a writer and as a historical researcher. Early in his move, he reached out to other writers and illustrators for children and young adults living in the area. This effort has yielded a friendship with author/artist Janet Stevens, who encouraged Avi in a project to serialize fiction with a local paper. When asked to describe his current home, Avi first reports with great animation and authority a brief history of Boulder, an area settled prior to the Civil War, a place that enjoyed a brief gold rush, and home to a state university in the late nineteenth century.

One of Boulder's attractions for Avi is the county's commitment to a "perpetual reserve" for the environment. A big creek that runs through the middle of Boulder continues to attract gold panners as well as kayakers, fishing enthusiasts, and swimmers. A running and biking path serves as such a major thoroughfare through town that it is cleared of snow throughout the winter.

Although Avi bemoans the cultural homogeneity of his new city of just over 100,000 and misses New England's evident ties to European diversity, he revels in the extensive support of the public library. He looks forward to celebrations of the arts and to the planned Shakespeare festival. Moreover, he enjoys the terrain's openness and distinctive geography. A gardener, he grows herbs and vegetables in his yard; as an athlete, he runs and recently bought a mountain bike and hopes to learn rollerblading. He quips that he fears expulsion from the state if he does not learn how to ski within the year.

Avi lives in a quiet neighborhood on Grove Street in half of a spacious 1910 brick house with "quirky" dimensions. A spiral staircase connects the first floor living space with the second floor. He enjoys a large living room, a kitchen, and the necessary home office. Like others in Boulder, he orients himself to the mountains. The mountain view from his window has already manifested itself in one of Avi's writing projects. This home sounds ideal for a cat, a pet Avi had in Providence. Even though he is not allowed a pet here, he keeps his doors open all the time and provides a dish of food for wandering felines. Avi hopes to equip his dark room with digital technology as he continues an avocation as a photographer.

Although Avi's Boulder location moves him away from his older brother, Henry, who lives outside of Boston, it does place him closer to his twin sister, Emily, who lives in California. Avi feels "very close to [his] brother and twin sister" and makes seeing them and fostering his relationships with them a continuing priority in his life. Growing up, Avi's "parents considered Henry a genius and lavished attention on him because of his academic achievements. Emily received a lot of parental attention and concern as a child because she had been born with a heart murmur. Emily was one of the first children in the United States to have open-heart surgery" (Markham, 39). Avi reports that he has few memories of his childhood and readily claims Emily as a more reliable source of their shared childhood than he is. Although fraternal twins, Avi and Emily maintained their own independence and developed individual personalities. Avi describes Emily as more sociable and outgoing throughout their growing up than he was. Although he recalls large family gatherings as exciting social events and frequent playtimes with his siblings and nearby cousins, Avi remembers himself often as outside the family circle, as a loner happy with his own creative thoughts. Avi "especially puzzles over [his parents'] failure to tell him that he had dysgraphia. If he had known he had a learning disability . . . perhaps . . . he would have felt better about himself. . . . When Avi asked his father why he and his mother hadn't told him about his disability as a child, his father replied that it had been his mother's decision not to tell him. By that time, Avi's mother was dead and could not provide Avi with an explanation" (Markham, 40).

The East Coast-West Coast spread of Avi's siblings mimics the geographical distance of Avi's now-adult sons: Shaun, a rock musician, lives in Boston; Kevin, a former performer who manages rock bands, resides in San Francisco; and his stepson, Gabriel, is a jour-

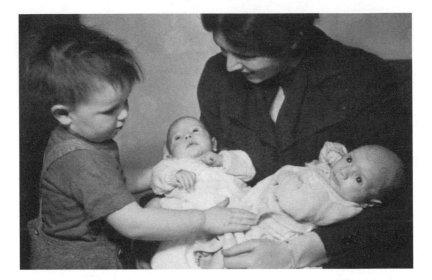

Henry and the twins Emily and Avi at the age of two months, held by their mother, Helen, in 1938.

nalist in Washington, D.C. Despite these varied locations, Avi keeps in touch with his family using today's technological conveniences, and he arranges to visit and spend time with them. Even as Avi expresses commitment to his role as a brother, his identity as a father genuinely excites him. He recalls the birth of his sons: "Shaun's birth had been very traditional, with Avi waiting outside the delivery room until the excitement was over. Much to Avi's delight, he was allowed to stay in the delivery room with Joan and to assist with Kevin's birth . . . a thrilling experience" (Markham, 58). Avi also values tremendously his relationship with his stepson, Gabriel. As Avi discusses his children, his listener not only detects tremendous parental pride but also discovers a father who so thoroughly invests himself in his parenting that he knows both when his offspring need support and when they need the independence to take risks. So much of Avi's fiction explores the nature, the nurture, the potential, and the obligations of fatherhood that it seems a keen, essential aspect of his selfhood.

Avi (left) with Emily and Henry.

With the birth of Ruby in 1996, Avi now adds grandfather to his familial roles. This new function may be startling to Avi, but what is not at all surprising to his audience is his bookish attention to this addition. As a birth gift, he sent Ruby a box of picture books, her first stories, and her first art. Avi suggested that this life experience may indeed return him to the picture book, a form of writing he has not done since his own children were young. Dis-

High school graduation portrait of Avi in 1954.

tance from Ruby limits Avi's interaction with her and, he says, prevents him from being able to talk extensively about grandparenting; however, he does enjoy hearing from her father, his son, Kevin, fresh stories and perspectives on fatherhood.

Current Projects

Some writers worry about running out of ideas for projects. Not so Avi, who juggles so many new projects simultaneously that one wonders when he finds time to eat and sleep, never mind to

Avi and sister Emily at the Alexander Book Company in San Francisco, 1992; photograph courtesy of Andree Abecassis.

socialize with the family and friends who are so important to him. He recently finished an I-Can-Read book with HarperCollins titled *Finding Providence: The Story of Roger Williams*. Here Avi joins serious content, the life of Roger Williams—which also becomes an exploration of the separation of church and state— with a challenging format. This book demonstrates Avi's belief in the ability of young readers not only to comprehend but also to be fully engaged with complex moral issues. Whereas Avi grew up in an atheistic household that celebrated the Jewish holidays for tradition's sake and Christian holidays for "cultural" reasons (Markham, 42), this book reflects Avi's great admiration for one who leads a religious life.

On first moving to Boulder, Avi began working on serializing fiction he was writing. Area newspapers were intrigued by this project and initially expressed interest. He set one of the pieces in Boulder and designed it for the children's pages of the paper. Although the idea fell through, it continues to hold interest for Avi.

Committed readers know well how few fantasies Avi has written. He believes one of the reasons he does not write as many fantasies as works of realistic fiction is that a sense of place, temporal and physical, are key to him as a writer. He has a difficult time imagining a place that does not exist and often relies on research as a tool for reconstructing place in his fiction. For example, in *The Fighting Ground*, Avi depended on historically accurate topographical maps to lend reality to his re-creation. Now, however, Avi is working on a fantasy of invented hobbitlike and hobbit-unlike creatures who ski. Still, place remains realistic; this time he is drawing on the mountain setting of Boulder, Colorado.

Avi wrote "Scout's Honor" for a short story collection edited by Amy Ehrlich at Candlewick Press titled *When I was Your Age*. Acknowledging that the short story form remains one of the most difficult to master, Avi adopts a single theme around which to join a series of eight short stories. The motif serves as a starting place, even as Avi reveals that "it may not end up that way." Coming on the heels of his longest book, the two-volume *Beyond the Western Sea*, this tight, compressed form poses unique challenges. Avi states that one tells a novel as far away from the end as possible, yet one writes a short story as close to the end as possible. Furthermore, in some ways, writing a short story is a bit like telling a joke well: It requires an inherent punch line defined throughout while the novel gathers disparate threads, ties them into a knot, and pulls. A short story "has to be perfect to be good." Not surprisingly, Avi deems *The Barn*, a self-contained novella, his most nearly perfect book.

Avi asks us to remember two crucial aspects that compose his attitude about writing. First, he finds it very difficult. Second, he loves doing it. Avi's readers may not witness the hardship of writing, but they relish the storytelling, the history, the magic, the style, the risk taking, the truthtelling, and the subversion of Avi's work.

Notes and References

Chapter One

1. E. M. Forster, *Aspects of the Novel* (New York: Harvest/Harcourt, Brace and Company, 1927), 40; hereafter cited in the text as *Aspects*.

2. Deborah Waldman, "Master Storyteller . . . Is it in the Genes?" *Jewish Voice of R. I.* (November 1995): 2; hereafter cited in the text as Waldman.

3. Avi, "From the Inside Out—The Author Speaks" (Publicity brochure from Bradbury Press, 1985).

4. Donald R. Gallo, ed., *Speaking for Ourselves* (Urbana, Ill.: National Council of Teachers of English, 1990), 13; hereafter cited as *Speaking*.

5. Anne Commire, ed., *Something about the Author,* vol. 14 (Detroit: Gale Research, 1987), 270.

6. Avi, unpublished interviews by Susan P. Bloom and Cathryn M. Mercier, tape recording, Boston, Mass., October 1995; telephone conversation, July 1996.

7. Sonia Benson, *Something about the Author,* vol. 71 (Detroit: Gale Research, 1993), 10.

8. Avi, *Things That Sometimes Happen* (New York: Doubleday, 1970), 76; hereafter cited in the text as *Things*.

9. *Kirkus Reviews* (1 December 1970): 1288.

10. Avi, *Snail Tale* (New York: Pantheon, 1972), 5; hereafter cited in the text as *Snail*.

11. Marianne Hough, *School Library Journal* (January 1973): 65.

12. Marjorie Fisher, *Growing Point* (October 1976): 2963.

13. Avi, *The Bird, the Frog, and the Light* (New York: Orchard, 1994), 13; hereafter cited in the text as *Bird*.

14. Drew Stevenson, *School Library Journal* (December 1980): 72.

15. Avi, *Who Stole the Wizard of Oz?* (New York: Knopf, 1981), 7.

16.   *Kirkus Reviews* (1 October 1981): 1235.

17.   Avi, *Romeo and Juliet—Together (and Alive!) at Last* (New York: Orchard, 1987), 42; hereafter cited in the text as *Romeo*.

18.   Barbara Elleman, *Booklist* (August 1987): 1740; hereafter cited in the text as Elleman.

19.   Lois Markham, *Avi* (Santa Barbara, Calif.: Learning Works, 1996), 82.

20.   Avi, *Wolf Rider: A Tale of Terror* (New York: Bradbury, 1985), 18; hereafter cited in the text as *Wolf*.

21.   Betsy Hearne, *Bulletin of the Center for Children's Books* (December 1986): 61; hereafter cited in the text as Hearne.

22.   Ruth Vose, *School Library Journal* (December 1986): 111–12; hereafter cited in the text as Vose.

23.   Carolyn Phelan, *Booklist* (15 October 1995): 402; hereafter cited in the text as Phelan.

24.   Avi, *Poppy* (New York: Orchard, 1995), 1; hereafter cited in the text as *Poppy*.

Chapter Two

1.   Naomi Shihab Nye, *This Same Sky* (New York: Four Winds Press, 1992), 57.

2.   Hazel Rochman, *Booklist* (15 January 1992): 930; hereafter cited in the text as Rochman.

3.   James S. Jacobs and Michael O. Tunnell, *Children's Literature Briefly* (New Jersey: Merrill/Prentice Hall, 1996), 80.

4.   Avi, *Blue Heron* (New York: Bradbury, 1992), 1; hereafter cited in the text as *Heron*.

5.   Avi, *Bright Shadow* (New York: Bradbury, 1985), 6; hereafter cited in the text as *Shadow*.

6.   Avi, *Tom, Babette, and Simon* (New York: Macmillan, 1995), 40; hereafter cited in the text as *Tom*.

7.   Roger Sutton, *Bulletin for the Center of Children's Books* (July/August 1995): 376–77.

8.   *Kirkus Reviews* (1 June 1995): 76–77.

9.   Cheri LaGuess Zarookian, *School Library Journal* (October 1975): 94; hereafter cited in the text as Zarookian.

Chapter Three

1.   Scott O'Dell, "History and Fiction," *Five Owls* (January/February 1990): 1.

2.   Perry Nodelman, *Pleasures of Children's Literature* (New York: Longman, 1996), 99; hereafter cited in the text as *Pleasures*.

3.   Sonia Benson, *Something about the Author,* vol. 71 (Detroit: Gale Research, 1993), 11; hereafter cited in the text as Benson.

4.   Donald R. Gallo, *Speaking for Ourselves* (Urbana, Ill.: National Council of Teachers of English, 1990), 14.

5.   Chuck Schacht, *School Library Journal* (April 1979): 52.

6.   Avi, *Night Journeys* (New York: Morrow, 1994), 3; hereafter cited in the text as *Night.*

7.   Ursula LeGuin, *Language of the Night* (New York: Putnam, 1979), 69.

8.   Avi, *Encounter at Easton* (New York: Morrow, 1994), 3; hereafter cited in the text as *Encounter.*

9.   Alethea K. Helbig and Agnes Regan Perkins, *Dictionary of American Children's Fiction 1960–1984: Recent Books of Recognized Merit* (Westport, Conn.: Greenwood Press, 1986), 195.

10.   A. Siaolys, *Best Sellers* (June 1980): 115.

11.   Avi, *Captain Grey* (New York: Morrow, 1993), 137; hereafter cited in the text as *Grey.*

12.   Jane O'Connor, *New York Times Book Review* (11 September 1977): 30.

13.   Elsa Marston, *Voice of Youth Advocates* (February 1985): 321.

14.   Avi, *The Fighting Ground* (New York: Lippincott, 1984), 10; hereafter cited in the text as *Fighting.*

15.   Zena Sutherland, *Bulletin of the Center for Children's Books* (June 1984): 180.

16.   Susan Stan, *Five Owls* (January/February 1990): 45.

17.   Barbara Ann Marinak, *Book Report* (March/April 1992): 26.

Chapter Four

1.   William Shakespeare, *A Midsummer Night's Dream,* 5.i.12–23.

2.   Avi, "Seeing through the I," *ALAN Review* (Spring 1993): 3–7; hereafter cited in the text as "Seeing."

3.   Sonia Benson, *Something about the Author,* vol. 71 (Detroit: Gale Research, 1993), 11.

4.   Cyrisse Jaffee, *School Library Journal* (March 1978): 124.

5.   Zena Sutherland, *Bulletin of the Center for Children's Books* (July/August 1978): 170.

6.   Alethea K. Helbig and Agnes Regan Perkins, *Dictionary of American Children's Fiction 1960–1984: Recent Books of Recognized Merit* (Westport, Conn.: Greenwood Press, 1986), 191; hereafter cited in the text as *Dictionary.*

7.   *Kirkus* (15 February 1981): 212.

8.   Zena Sutherland, *Bulletin of the Center for Children's Books* (November 1980): 46; hereafter cited in the text as Sutherland 1980.

9.   Barbara Elleman, *Booklist* (15 December 1980): 569.
10.   Avi, unpublished interviews by Susan P. Bloom and Cathryn M. Mercier, tape recording, Boston, Mass., October 1995; telephone conversation, July 1996.
11.   Avi, *Emily Upham's Revenge; Or, How Deadwood Dick Saved the Day* (New York: Morrow, 1993), 24; hereafter cited in the text as *Emily.*
12.   Avi, "Children's Literature: The American Revolution," *Top of the News* (Winter 1977): 160.
13.   Avi, *The History of Helpless Harry: To Which is Added a Variety of Amusing and Entertaining Adventures* (New York: Morrow, 1995), 3; hereafter cited in the text as *Harry.*
14.   Avi, *Children's Literature Review,* vol. 24 (Detroit: Gale Research, 1991), 2.
15.   *Kirkus* (1 August 1988): 1145.
16.   Avi, *Something Upstairs* (New York: Orchard, 1990), 12; hereafter cited in the text as *Upstairs.*
17.   Michael Cart, *School Library Journal* (October 1988): 143.
18.   Hannah Zeiger, *Horn Book* (January/February 1989): 65.
19.   Patricia Waugh, *Metafiction: The Theory and Practice of Self-Conscious Fiction* (New York: Methuen, 1984), 2.
20.   Avi, *The Man Who Was Poe* (New York: Orchard, 1989), 20; hereafter cited in the text as *Poe.*
21.   Robert Alter, *Partial Magic: The Novel as a Self-Conscious Genre* (Berkeley, Calif.: University of California Press, 1975), xi.
22.   Roger Sutton, *Bulletin of the Center for Children's Books* (October 1989): 27.
23.   Elizabeth S. Watson, *Horn Book* (March/April 1990): 205; hereafter cited in the text as Watson.
24.   Susan Stan, *Five Owls* (January/February 1990): 45.

Chapter Five

1.   Lewis Carroll, *Alice's Adventures in Wonderland* (London: Puffin Books, 1962; original publication, 1866, London: Macmillan and Co. Ltd.), 23.
2.   Roger Sutton, *Bulletin of the Center for Children's Books* (October 1993): 37; hereafter cited in the text as Sutton.
3.   Avi, *City of Light, City of Dark* (New York: Orchard, 1993), 91; hereafter cited in the text as *City.*
4.   Avi, unpublished interviews by Susan P. Bloom and Cathryn M. Mercier, tape recording, Boston, Mass., October 1995; telephone conversation, July 1996.
5.   Jon Peters, *School Library Journal* (September 1993): 228.
6.   Susan P. Bloom, *Five Owls* (November/December 1992): 40.
7.   Maeve Visser Knoth, *Horn Book* (March/April 1993): 205.

8. Avi, *"Who Was That Masked Man, Anyway?"* (New York: Orchard, 1992), 13–14; hereafter cited in the text as *Masked.*
9. Avi, "Seeing through the I," *ALAN Review* (Spring 1993): 6; hereafter cited in the text as "Seeing."
10. Hazel Rochman, *Booklist* (August 1992): 2012.
11. *Kirkus* (1 August 1992): 986.
12. Judith Rovenger, *New York Times Book Review* (2 March 1992): 21; hereafter cited in the text as Rovenger.
13. Sonia Benson, *Something about the Author,* vol. 71 (Detroit: Gale Research, 1993), 13.
14. Elizabeth S. Watson, *Horn Book* (January 1992): 78.
15. Avi, *Nothing but the Truth* (New York: Orchard, 1991), i; hereafter cited in the text as *Truth.*
16. *Nothing but the Truth,* i.

Chapter Six

1. Samuel L. Clemens (Mark Twain), *The Adventures of Huckleberry Finn,* eds. Sculley Bradley, Richmond Croom Beatty, and E. Hudson Long (New York: Norton, 1961), 7.
2. Ursula B. LeGuin, "The Child and the Shadow," in *The Language of the Night* (New York: Berkley, 1982), 60; hereafter cited in the text as "Shadow."
3. Avi, *Sometimes I Think I Hear My Name* (New York: Pantheon, 1982), 3; hereafter cited in the text as *Name.*
4. Ilene Cooper, *Booklist* (1 June 1982): 1308; hereafter cited in the text as Cooper.
5. Avi, "Writing Books for Young People," in *The Writer* (March 1982): 18–20, 28.
6. Avi, *Devil's Race* (New York: Lippincott, 1984), 6; hereafter cited in the text as *Race.*
7. Patricia A. Morgans, *Best Sellers* (December 1984): 356.
8. Jack Forman, *School Library Journal* (October 1984): 164.
9. Avi, "Seeing through the I," *ALAN Review* (Spring 1993): 6.
10. Virginia Hamilton, "Ah, Sweet Rememory," in *Innocence and Experience: Essays and Conversations in Children's Literature,* eds. Barbara Harrison and Gregory Maguire (New York: Lothrop, 1987), 6.
11. Avi, *The True Confessions of Charlotte Doyle* (New York: Orchard, 1990), 3; hereafter cited in the text as *Charlotte.*
12. Mary M. Burns, *Horn Book* (January/February 1991): 65.
13. Avi, "The Inside Story: *The True Confessions of Charlotte Doyle,*" *Book Links* (15 February 1991): 1225–26; hereafter cited in the text as *Book Links.*
14. Trev Jones, *School Library Journal* (September 1990): 224.

15.   Cathryn M. Mercier, *Five Owls* (January/February 1991): 56–57.
16.   Avi, "Boston Globe-Horn Book Award Acceptance Speech," *Horn Book* (January/February 1992): 26; hereafter cited in the text as "Boston Globe."

Chapter Seven

1.   Charles Dickens, *Oliver Twist* (New York: Penguin Books, 1966; first published 1838), 35.
2.   Avi, "The Child in Children's Literature," *Horn Book* (January/February 1993): 48; hereafter cited in the text as "Child."
3.   Avi, "Scout's Honor," in *When I Was Your Age*, ed. Amy Ehrlich (Boston: Candlewick, 1996), 122–39.
4.   Mary M. Burns, *Horn Book* (January/February 1995): 49; hereafter cited in the text as Burns.
5.   Avi, *S.O.R. Losers* (New York: Bradbury, 1984), 5; hereafter cited in the text as *S.O.R.*
6.   Avi, *Windcatcher* (New York: Bradbury, 1991), 34; hereafter cited in the text as *Windcatcher*.
7.   Nancy Vasilakis, *Horn Book* (May/June 1991): 329.
8.   Hazel Rochman, *Booklist* (1 March 1991): 1382–83.
9.   Bryna J. Fireside, *New York Times Book Review* (1 March 1981): 24.
10.   Avi, *A Place Called Ugly* (New York: Pantheon, 1981), 10–11; hereafter cited in the text as *Place*.
11.   Virginia Haviland, *Horn Book* (June 1981): 298.
12.   Avi, *Shadrach's Crossing* (New York: Pantheon, 1983), 34–35; hereafter cited in the text as *Shadrach*.
13.   *Kirkus* (15 June 1983): 662; hereafter cited in the text as *Kirkus*.
14.   Alethea K. Helbig and Agnes Regan Perkins, *Dictionary of American Children's Fiction 1960–1984: Recent Books of Recognized Merit* (Westport, Conn.: Greenwood, 1986), 590; hereafter cited in the text as *Dictionary*.
15.   Kate M. Flanagan, *Horn Book* (August 1983): 440.
16.   Linda Wicher, *School Library Journal* (August 1983): 61.
17.   Avi, unpublished interviews by Susan P. Bloom and Cathryn M. Mercier, tape recording, Boston, Mass., October 1995; telephone conversation, July 1996.

Chapter Eight

1.   Leo Tolstoy, *Anna Karenina* (New York: New American Library, 1961; first published 1877), 17.
2.   Stephanie Coontz, *The Way We Never Were: American Families and the Nostalgia Trap* (New York: BasicBooks, 1992).

3. Avi, *Punch with Judy* (New York; Bradbury, 1993), 9; hereafter cited in the text as *Punch*.

4. Sally Margolis, *School Library Journal* (June 1993): 102.

5. Ilene Cooper, *Booklist* (15 March 1993): 1312.

6. Elizabeth Huntoon, *Horn Book* (July/August 1993): 341.

7. Hazel Rochman, *Booklist* (1 September 1994): 40; hereafter cited in the text as Rochman.

8. Ellen Fader, *Horn Book* (January/February 1995): 57.

9. Avi, *The Barn* (New York: Orchard, 1994), 7; hereafter cited in the text as *Barn*.

10. Avi, *Beyond the Western Sea. Book One: The Escape from Home* (New York: Orchard, 1996), 31; hereafter cited in the text as *Escape*.

11. Hazel Rochman, *Booklist* (1 February 1996): 930; hereafter cited in the text as Rochman 1996.

12. Roger Sutton, *Bulletin of the Center for Children's Books* (February 1996): 183.

Chapter Nine

1. Avi, in conversation with Richard Jackson at Simmons College, "A Room of One's Own" Summer Institute, 25 July 1995; unpublished.

2. Richard Jackson, "We," *Horn Book* (May/June 1993): 296–302.

Chapter Ten

1. Avi, "Writing Books for Young People," *The Writer* (March 1982): 18; hereafter cited in the text as "Writing."

2. Avi, unpublished interviews by Susan P. Bloom and Cathryn M. Mercier, tape recording, Boston, Mass., October 1995; telephone conversation, July 1996. A significant portion of additional material in this chapter—having to do with Avi's personal life and writing habits—comes from these sessions.

3. Deborah Waldman, *Jewish Voice of R. I.* (November 1995): 17; hereafter cited in the text as Waldman.

4. Avi, "Making the Most of a School Visit: Ideas, Suggestions, Hopes" (1991), 1; hereafter cited in the text as "Visit."

5. *The American Heritage Stedman's Medical Dictionary* (Boston: Houghton, 1995), 247.

6. Lois Markham, *Avi* (Santa Barbara, Calif.: Learning Works, 1996), 82.

7. Natalie Babbitt, letter to Susan P. Bloom, November 8, 1995.

8. Avi, "The Inside Story: *The True Confessions of Charlotte Doyle*," *Book Links* (15 February 1991): 1226; hereafter cited in the text as *Book Links*.

9. Barbara Elleman, *Book Links* (January 1992): 60–61.

Selected Bibliography

Primary Sources

Young Adult Novels

A Place Called Ugly. New York: Pantheon, 1981; Scholastic, 1982; Avon, 1994.

Sometimes I Think I Hear My Name. New York: Pantheon, 1982; New American Library, 1983; Avon, 1995.

Shadrach's Crossing. New York: Pantheon, 1983; (retitled *Smuggler's Island*) Morrow, 1994; Beech Tree, 1994.

Devil's Race. New York: Lippincott, 1984; Avon, 1987.

Bright Shadow. New York: Bradbury, 1985.

Wolf Rider: A Tale of Terror. New York: Bradbury, 1985; Aladdin, 1988.

Something Upstairs. New York: Orchard, 1988; Avon, 1990.

The Man Who Was Poe. New York: Orchard, 1989; Avon, 1991.

The True Confessions of Charlotte Doyle. New York: Orchard, 1990; Avon, 1992.

Nothing but the Truth. New York: Orchard, 1991; Avon, 1993.

Blue Heron. New York: Bradbury, 1992; Avon, 1993.

"Who Was That Masked Man, Anyway?" New York: Orchard, 1992; Avon, 1994.

City of Light, City of Dark. New York: Orchard, 1993; Orchard, 1995.

Punch with Judy. New York: Bradbury, 1993.

Beyond the Western Sea
  Book One: The Escape from Home. New York: Orchard, 1996.
  Book Two: Lord Kirkle's Money. New York: Orchard, 1996.

Children's Books

Snail Tale. New York: Pantheon, 1972.

No More Magic. New York: Pantheon, 1975; Bantam, 1979; Beech Tree, 1995.

Captain Grey. New York: Pantheon, 1977; Bantam, 1978; reissued New York: Morrow Junior Books, 1993.

Emily Upham's Revenge; Or, How Deadwood Dick Saved the Day. New York: Pantheon, 1978; Bantam, 1978; Beech Tree, 1993; Morrow, 1993.

Night Journeys. New York: Pantheon, 1979; Scholastic, 1981; Beech Tree, 1994; Morrow, 1994.

Encounter at Easton. New York: Pantheon, 1980; Beech Tree, 1994; Morrow, 1994.

The History of Helpless Harry: To Which is Added a Variety of Amusing and Entertaining Adventures. New York: Pantheon, 1980; Beech Tree, 1995; Morrow, 1995.

Man from the Sky. New York: Knopf, 1980.

Who Stole the Wizard of Oz? New York: Knopf, 1981, 1990.

The Fighting Ground. New York: Lippincott, 1984; HarperTrophy, 1987.

S.O.R. Losers. New York: Bradbury, 1984; Avon, 1986.

Romeo and Juliet Together (and Alive!) at Last. New York: Orchard, 1987; Avon, 1988.

Windcatcher. New York: Bradbury, 1991.

The Barn. New York: Orchard, 1994.

Poppy. New York: Orchard, 1995.

Tom, Babette, & Simon. New York: Macmillan, 1995.

Picture Books

Things That Sometimes Happen: Very Short Stories for Very Young Readers. New York: Doubleday, 1970.

The Bird, the Frog, and the Light. New York: Orchard, 1994.

Finding Providence: The Story of Roger Williams. New York: Harper-Collins, 1997.

Short Stories for Children

"Scout's Honor," in *When I Was Your Age,* ed. Amy Ehrlich. Cambridge, Mass.: Candlewick Press, 1996.

Speeches and Articles

"Children's Literature: The American Revolution." *Top of the News* (Winter 1977): 149–61.

"When Authors Visit Schools: A Symposium." *Children's Literature in Education* (Autumn 1980): 145–46.

"Writing Books for Young People." *The Writer* (March 1982): 18–20, 28.

"Some Thoughts on the YA World." *Voice of Youth Advocates* (October 1984): 183–84.

"Reviewing the Reviewers." *School Library Journal* (March 1986): 114–15.

"School Visits: The Author's Viewpoint," coauthor Betty Miles. *School Library Journal* (January 1987): 21–26.

"All That Glitters." *Horn Book* (September/October 1987): 569–76.

"Robert Lawson." *Writers for Children: Critical Studies of Major Authors since the Seventeenth Century,* ed. Jane M. Bingham. New York: Scribner's, 1987.

"The Inside Story: *The True Confessions of Charlotte Doyle. Book Links* (15 February 1991): 1225–30.

"Making the Most of a School Visit: Ideas, Suggestions, Hopes." copyright Avi, 1991.

Acceptance Speech for *The Boston Globe-Horn Book* Fiction Award for *The True Confessions of Charlotte Doyle, Horn Book* (January/February 1992): 24–27.

"The Child in Children's Literature." *Horn Book* (January/ February 1993): 40–50.

"Seeing through the I." *ALAN Review* (Spring 1993): 3–7.

"Young People, Books, and the Right to Read." *Journal of Youth Services in Libraries* (Spring 1993): 245–56.

"I can read, I can read!" *Horn Book* (March/April 1994): 166–69.

Secondary Sources

Books and Parts of Books

Benson, Sonia. *Something about the Author,* vol. 71, ed. Diane Teligen. Detroit: Gale Research, 1993.

Children's Literature Review, vol. 24, ed. Gerald J. Senick. Detroit: Gale Research, 1991.

Gallo, Donald R., ed. *Speaking for Ourselves.* Urbana, Ill.: National Council of Teachers of English, 1990.

Markham, Lois. *Avi.* Santa Barbara, Calif.: Learning Works, 1996.

Moss, Anita. *Twentieth Century Children's Writers,* 3d ed., ed. Tracy Chevalier. Detroit: St. James Press, 1989.

Sieruta, Peter D. *Children's Books and Their Creators,* ed. Anita Silvey. Boston: Houghton Mifflin, 1995.

Something about the Author, vol. 14, ed. Anne Comire. Detroit: Gale Research, 1987.

Strickland, Robbie W. *Twentieth Century Young Adult Writers,* ed. Laura Standley Berger. Detroit: St. James Press, 1994.

Articles

Jackson, Richard. "We." *Horn Book* (May/June 1993): 296–302.

Stan, Susan. "Conversations: Avi." *Five Owls* (January/February 1990): 45.

Interviews

Marinak, Barbara Ann. "Author Profile: Avi." *Book Report* (March/April 1992): 26–28.

Selected Book Reviews

A Place Called Ugly

Fireside, Bryna J. *New York Times Book Review* (1 March 1981): 24.
Lewis, Marjorie. *School Library Journal* (8 April 1981): 136.
Kirkus Reviews (1 April 1981): 436.

The Barn

Banks, Ann. *New York Times Book Review* (1 January 1995): 15.
Engelfried, Steven. *School Library Journal* (October 1994): 118.
Kirkus Reviews (15 October 1994): 1404.
Rochman, Hazel. *Booklist* (1 September 1994): 40.

Beyond the Western Sea. Book One: The Escape from Home

Publishers Weekly (1 April 1996): 77.
Hazel Rochman. *Booklist* (1 February 1996): 930.
Roger Sutton. *Bulletin of the Center for Children's Books* (February 1996): 183.

The Bird, the Frog and the Light

Corsaro, Julie. *Booklist* (15 April 1994): 1536.
Sutton, Roger. *Bulletin for the Center of Children's Books* (February 1994): 180–81.
Wilton, Shirley. *School Library Journal* (April 1994): 95.

Blue Heron

Kirkus Reviews (15 January 1992): 112.
Rochman, Hazel. *Booklist* (15 January 1992): 930.
Sutton, Roger. *Bulletin of the Center for Children's Books* (June 1992): 253–54.

Bright Shadow

Smith, Karen P. *School Library Journal* (December 1985): 86; *Bulletin of the Center for Children's Books* (February 1986): 102.

Captain Grey

O'Connor, Jane. *New York Times Book Review* (11 September 1977): 30.
Stoiaken, Larry. *Best Sellers* (June 1977): 94.

City of Light, City of Dark: A Comic-Book Novel

Del Negro, Janice. *Booklist* (15 September 1993): 142.
Peters, Jon. *School Library Journal* (September 1993): 228.
Sutton, Roger. *Bulletin for the Center of Children's Books* (October 1993): 37.

Devil's Race

Forman, Jack. *School Library Journal* (October 1984): 164.
Morgans, Patricia A. *Best Sellers* (December 1984): 356.

Emily Upham's Revenge; Or, How Deadwood Dick Saved the Day

Helbig, Alethea K., and Agnes Regan Perkins. *Dictionary of American Children's Fiction, 1960–1984: Recent Recognized Books of Merit* (Westport, Conn.: Greenwood, 1986).
Jaffee, Cyrisse. *School Library Journal* (March 1987): 124.
Sutherland, Zena. *Bulletin of the Center for Children's Books* (July 1987): 170.

Encounter at Easton

Elleman, Barbara. *Booklist* (15 June 1980): 1528.
Geringer, Laura. *School Library Journal* (May 1980): 64.
Helbig, Alethea K., and Agnes Regan Perkins. *Dictionary of American Children's Fiction, 1960–1984: Recent Recognized Books of Merit* (Westport, Conn.: Greenwood, 1986).

The Fighting Ground

Hanley, Karen Stang. *Booklist* (1 June 1984): 1395–96.
Marcus, Susan F. *School Library Journal* (September 1984): 125.
Marston, Elsa. *Voice of Youth Advocates* (February 1985): 321.
Sutherland, Zena. *Bulletin of the Center for Children's Books* (June 1984): 180.
Taxel, Joel. *ALAN Review* (Spring 1985): 23.

The History of Helpless Harry: To Which Is Added a Variety of Amusing and Entertaining Adventures

Elleman, Barbara. *Booklist* (15 December 1980).

Kirkus Reviews (15 February 1981): 212.
Sutherland, Zena. *Bulletin of the Center for Children's Books* (November 1980): 46.

Man from the Sky

Goldberger, Judith. *Booklist* (15 July 1980): 1678.
Stevenson, Drew. *School Library Journal* (December 1980): 72.

The Man Who Was Poe

Kirkus Reviews (1 October 1989): 1470.
Shook, Bruce Ann. *School Library Journal* (September 1989): 271–72.
Watson, Elizabeth S. *Horn Book* (March 1990): 205.

Night Journeys

Kirkus Reviews (1 May 1979): 517.
Schacht, Chuck. *School Library Journal* (April 1979): 52.
Sutherland, Zena. *Bulletin of the Center for Children's Books* (September 1979): 2.

No More Magic

Helbig, Alethea K., and Agnes Regan Perkins. *Dictionary of American Children's Fiction, 1960–1984: Recent Books of Recognized Merit* (Westport, Conn.: Greenwood Press, 1986), 476.
Zarookian, Cherie LaGuess. *School Library Journal* (October 1975): 94.

Nothing but the Truth

Elleman, Barbara. *Book Links* (January 1992): 60–61.
Fader, Ellen. *School Library Journal* (January 1992): 36–37.
Kirkus Reviews (1 October 1991: 1284; 15 September 1992: 1346).
Rovenger, Judith. *New York Times Book Review* (2 March 1992): 21.
Sutton, Roger. *Bulletin for the Center of Children's Books* (September 1991): 2.
Watson, Elizabeth S. *Horn Book* (January 1992): 78.
Zvirin, Stephanie. *Booklist* (15 September 1991): 136.

Poppy

Flowers, Ann A. *Horn Book* (January/February 1996): 70–71.
Publisher's Weekly (21 August 1995): 66.

Punch with Judy

Cooper, Ilene. *Booklist* (15 March 1993): 1312.

Huntoon, Elizabeth. *Bulletin of the Center for Children's Books* (July 1993): 341.
Kirkus Reviews (15 April 1993): 523–24.
Margolis, Sally. *School Library Journal* (June 1993): 102.

Romeo and Juliet—Together (and Alive!) at Last

Elleman, Barbara. *Booklist* (August 1987): 1740.
Kirkus Reviews (1 July 1987): 987.
Publisher's Weekly (28 August 1987): 81.

Shadrach's Crossing

Kirkus Reviews (15 June 1983): 662.
Flanagan, Kate M. *Horn Book* (August 1983): 439–40.
Wicher, Linda. *School Library Journal* (August 1983): 61.

Something Upstairs: A Tale of Ghosts

Kirkus Reviews (1 August 1988): 1145–46.
Sutton, Roger. *Bulletin of the Center for Children's Books* (September 1988): 2.
Zeiger, Hanna B. *Horn Book* (January 1989): 65.

Sometimes I Think I Hear My Name

Anderson, H. T. *Best Sellers* (May 1982): 76.
Cooper, Ilene. *Booklist* (1 June 1982): 1308.
Hains, Maryellen. *ALAN Review* (Fall 1982): 19.

S.O.R. Losers

Burns, Mary M. *Horn Book* (January 1985): 49.
Cooper, Ilene. *Booklist* (15 October 1984): 303.

Things That Sometimes Happen: Very Short Stories for Very Young Readers

Kirkus Reviews (1 December 1970): 1288.
Lewis, Marjorie. *School Library Journal* (March 1971): 116.

Tom, Babette, and Simon

Estes, Cheri. *School Library Journal* (June 1995): 108.
Kirkus Reviews (1 June 1995): 776.
Phelan, Carolyn. *Booklist* (15 May 1995): 1643.
Sutton, Roger. *Bulletin of the Center for Children's Books* (July 1995): 376–77.

The True Confessions of Charlotte Doyle

Burns, Mary M. *Horn Book* (January 1991): 65–66.
Elleman, Barbara. *Booklist* (1 September 1991): 44.
Jones, Trev. *School Library Journal* (September 1990): 221.
Kirkus Reviews (1 October 1990): 1390.
Mercier, Cathryn. *Five Owls* (January/February 1991): 56–57.
Sutherland, Zena. *Bulletin for the Center of Children's Books* (November 1990): 53.

Who Stole the Wizard of Oz?

Kirkus Reviews (1 October 1981): 1235.

"Who Was That Masked Man, Anyway?"

Bloom, Susan P. *Five Owls* (November/December 1992): 40–41.
Knoth, Maeve Visser. *Horn Book* (March/April 1993): 205.
Rochman, Hazel. *Booklist* (15 August 1992): 2012.
Sutton, Roger. *Bulletin of the Center for Children's Books* (October 1992): 35.

Windcatcher

Chatton, Barbara. *School Library Journal* (April 1991): 116.
Jennings, Katharine Pierson. *Bulletin of the Center for Children's Books* (May 1991): 210.
Kirkus Reviews (15 February 1991): 224.
Rochman, Hazel. *Booklist* (1 March 1991): 1382–83.
Vasilakis, Nancy. *Horn Book* (May 1991): 329–30.

Wolf Rider: A Tale of Terror

Elleman, Barbara. *Booklist* (15 November 1986): 505–6.
Hearne, Betsy. *Bulletin of the Center for Children's Books* (December 1986): 61.
Vose, Ruth S. *School Library Journal* (December 1986): 111–12.

Appendix

Recordings

Blue Heron, Recorded Books.
The Fighting Ground, Listening Library and Recorded Books.
Something Upstairs, Recorded Books.
The True Confessions of Charlotte Doyle, Recorded Books.
Who Was That Masked Man, Anyway? Recorded Books.
Wolf Rider, Recorded Books.

Performed on "Read to Me," Maine Public Radio

Emily Upham's Revenge
The Fighting Ground
Nothing but the Truth
Shadrach's Crossing
Something Upstairs
The True Confessions of Charlotte Doyle

Awards and Citations

The Barn
American Booksellers, Pick of the Lists, 1994

The Bird, the Frog, and the Light
American Booksellers, Pick of the Lists, 1994

Blue Heron
American Library Association, Best Books for Young Adult List, 1993
New York Public Library, *Books for the Teen Age,* 1993.

City of Light, City of Dark: A Comic-Book Novel
Publishers Weekly Best Children's Books of the Year, 1993
New York Public Library, *Books for the Teen Age,* 1994

Emily Upham's Revenge
Mystery Writers of America, Special Award, 1979

Encounter at Easton
Christopher Award, 1980

The Fighting Ground
American Library Association, Notable, 1984
American Library Association, Best Books for Young Adults, 1984
Bologna, International Book Fair, White Raven, 1984
National Council of Teachers of English, Notable Children's Trade Book in Social Studies, 1984
Scott O'Dell Award, Best Historical Fiction, 1984
Virginia Library Association, Jefferson Cup Award, Honor Book, 1985

The Man from the Sky
International Reading Association, Children's Choice, 1980

The Man Who Was Poe
Library of Congress, Best Books of the Year, 1990
Mystery Writers of America, nomination for Best Juvenile Mystery of the Year, 1990
National Council of Teachers of English, Notable Children's Book, 1990
New York Public Library, Best Books of the Year, 1989

Night Journeys
School Library Journal, Best Books of the Year, 1980

No More Magic
Mystery Writers of America, Special Award, 1975

Nothing but the Truth
Booklist Editors' Choice, 1991
Bulletin of the Center for Children's Books, Blue Ribbon Book, 1991
National Council of Social Studies/Children's Book Council, Notable, 1991
Publishers Weekly Best Books of 1991
American Booksellers Children's Choice List, 1992
American Library Association Notable, 1992
Bank Street Teachers' College, Best Books of the Year List, 1992
Boston Globe-Horn Book Award Honor Book, 1992

194   *Appendix*

Horn Book Fanfare, 1992
Library of Congress, Best Books for Children, 1992
National Council of Teachers of English, Notable Children's Trade Book
    in the Language Arts, 1992
New York Public Library, Best Books for Teens, 1992
Newbery Honor Book, 1992
Young Adult Services Division (of the American Library Association),
    Best Books for Young Adults, 1992
Arizona Young Readers' Award, 1994
New York State Readers' Award, 1994

Romeo and Juliet—Together (and Alive!) at Last
American Library Association/Young Adult Services Division, Recom-
    mended Book for Reluctant Readers, 1988
Bank Street Teachers' College, Children's Book Committee, Best Books
    of the Year, 1988
Child Study Association Book of the Year, 1988
International Reading Association, Children's Choice, 1988
Wisconsin Children's Book Center, Best Books of the Year, 1988

Shadrach's Crossing
Mystery Writers of America, Special Award, 1983

Snail Tale
British Book Council, Best Books of the Year, 1973

S.O.R. Losers
Parents' Choice, Remarkable Books, 1984
New York Public Library, Best Books, 1984

Something Upstairs
Library of Congress, Best Books of the Year, 1989
Mystery Writers of America, nomination for Best Juvenile Mystery of the
    Year, 1989
Rhode Island Award, 1991
Florida Sunshine Award, 1992
California Young Readers' Award, 1993

The True Confessions of Charlotte Doyle
American Library Association Notable, 1990
Booklist Editors' Choice, 1990

Child Study Association, Best Books, 1990
Golden Kite Award, 1990
International Reading Association, Children's Choice, 1990
New York Public Library, Best Books for Teens, 1990
School Library Journal, Best Books of 1990
Boston Globe-Horn Book Award, 1991
English Journal, Honors List, 1991
Horn Book, Fanfare, 1991
Library of Congress, *100 Best Books for Children,* 1991
Lopez Memorial Foundation Award (by the Los Angeles Chapter of the
    Women's National Book Association), 1991
National Council of Teachers of English, Notable Children's Trade Book
    in the Language Arts, 1991
Newbery Honor Book, 1991
Young Adult Services Division of the American Library Association, Best
    Books for Young Adults, 1991
Utah Young Adult Award, 1994

"Who Was That Masked Man, Anyway?"
Booklist Editors' Choice, 1992
New York Public Library, *Children's Books: One Hundred Titles for
    Reading and Sharing,* 1992.
School Library Journal Best Book, 1992
American Booksellers Pick of the List, 1993
American Library Association Notable, 1993

Windcatcher
Bank Street Teachers' College, Best Books of the Year List, 1991

Wolf Rider
American Library Association, Best Books for Young Adults, 1986
American Library Association/Young Adult Services Division, Recom-
    mended Book for Reluctant Readers, 1986
Booklist, Best Books of the Eighties, 1989
American Library Association/Young Adult Services Division, Mystery
    Genre Book List, 1990

Index

200 *Index*

fantasy, 17, 23. See also *Bright
Shadow; City of Light, City of Dark;
Snail Tale: The Adventures of a
Rather Small Snail; Tom, Babette,
and Simon*
farce, 57. See also mimicry; parody;
satire; spoof
Farnlee. Mr. *(Revenge)*, 55
father, 29; death of, 131, 133, 137; per-
ceptions of, 29, 93, 136; saving, 73
Father *(Barn)*, 135–40
father/daughter relationship, 19, 23,
25, 31
father figure, 37, 47, 104, 130–31,
141–42. See also Corporal; Da; Jaggery, Captain; Shinn, Everett
father/son: activities, 5–7; communication, 13–14, 15–16; relationship,
13–14, 15–16, 93. See also father
figure
feather, of heron, 27
Fenton, Ann *(Race)*, 96, 98, 100
Fenton, Nora *(Race)*, 96–97
fiction, reality vs., 63–65, 76. See also
metafiction
Fighting Ground, The, xii, 36, 47–50,
62, 135, 163, 176; Scott O'Dell Award
for Historical Fiction (1985), 50
*Finding Providence: The Story of
Roger Williams*, xvii, 175
Fisher, Margery, 8
Floca, Brian, 70–72
foreshadowing, 19, 103, 139
Forster, E. M. , 1, 22
Fred *(Escape)*, 146
freedom: bird as symbol of, 30; dancing as symbol of, 21

Gabriel (Avi's step-son), 172
Gainer, Joan, xv, 169
Gareth *(Shadow)*, 25
Garfield, Leon, 52
German, 48
Ghost. See Caleb; Proud, John (ghost
in *Race*)
ghost story, 36, 60, 63, 95. See also
*Devil's Race; Something Upstairs:
A Tale of Ghosts*

Gillian *(Sky)*, 9–10
Goddard, Ed *(Sky)*, 9–10
Golden Bird *(Tom)*, 29–30, 33
Gomez, Miss *(Masked)*, 78. See also
Wattleson, Mrs.
good, evil vs., 43, 70, 73–74, 89, 95
Grahame, Kenneth, *The Wind in the
Willows*, 16
greed, 27, 29, 33, 38, 58
Green Hornet, 76
Green Lantern, 30
Grey, Captain *(Grey)*, 43–47, 48. See
also Linnly, Robert
Grey, Mr. *(Encounter)*, 42–43
Griffen, Ted *(Truth)*, 85
Grummage *(Charlotte)*, 102

Hamlet, 142–43
Hansel & Gretel, 42, 44, 67
Hardy Boys, 75
HarperCollins, 175
Harrison *(Barn)*, 135–38
Harry *(Harry)*, 55–58
Hearne, Betsy, 16
Helga, Miss *(Shadow)*, 24
heroism, nature of, 79
Herold, Maggie, 162
Heron, xiii, 26–28, 30–32, 119; as
omen, 26–27
Hessians *(Fighting)*, 47–49
Hill, Nathaniel *(Encounter)*,
41–42, 43
historical fiction, xvi, 35–36, 50, 51.
See also *Barn, The; Beyond the
Western Sea; Captain Grey; Emily
Upham's Revenge; or, How Dead-
wood Dick Saved the Banker's
Niece; Encounter at Easton; Fight-
ing Ground, The; History of Help-
less Harry: To Which Is Added a
Variety of Amusing and Entertain-
ing Adventures; Man Who Was Poe,
The; Night Journeys; Shadrach's
Crossing; True Confessions of
Charlotte Doyle, The*
historicize, dehistoricize vs., 36, 50, 51
*History of Helpless Harry: To Which
Is Added a Variety of Amusing and*

Malloy, Philip *(Truth),* 82–88 166
Man from the Sky, The, xvi, 9–10, 117
Man Who Was Poe, The, xiii, xvii, 36,
    51, 63–69, 71, 109, 135
Mann, Thomas, 149
Mario *(Masked),* 75–77
Markham, Lois, 166, 169–72
Marple, Seth *(Revenge),* 52–55, 58
Marryat, Mr. *(Revenge),* 52
mask, as metaphor, 51, 66, 79
masquerade, 90–91, 94–95, 104
"Masquerade" (conference), 51
matrilineage, 72
Mawes, Elizabeth *(Night
    &Encounter),* 37–39, 41–42, 43, 110
McPhearson, Miss *(Stole)* , 10
McSneed, Joe *(Punch),* 130–31, 133
McSneed, Judy *(Punch),* 130–34
McSneed, Molly *(Punch),* 130–31, 134
melodrama, 12–13, 36. See also *Emily
    Upham's Revenge; or, How Dead-
    wood Dick Saved the Banker's
    Niece; History of Helpless Harry: To
    Which Is Added a Variety of Amus-
    ing and Entertaining Adventures;*
    Victorian novel
Mercier, Cathryn, 109
Merlin the Magician, 28, 29
Merry Men *(Punch),* 130, 132, 133
metafiction, 7, 56, 57, 63–64. *See also*
    fiction, reality vs.
Michael (Avi's cousin), 4, 75
"Midsummer Night's Dream, A," 51
Mike *(Magic),* 33
mimicry, 56. *See also* farce; parody;
    satire; spoof
Money Island, 116
moral ambiguity, 33, 38, 47, 140
Morwenna *(Shadow),* 24–26, 27, 33,
    61, 65, 110
Mother *(Barn),* 135, 137
*Mrs. E. P. Miller's Mother Truth's
    Melodies: Common Sense for Chil-
    dren,* 58
Muffin *(Magic),* 30–31
multiculturalism, 74
"Murders at the Rue Morgue," 64
My Brother Sam is Dead, 50

Myers, Walter Dean, 163
mystery, 10, 64, 66–68, 73, 116–17,
    125. See also *Man from the Sky,
    The; Man Who Was Poe, The;
    Something Upstairs: A Tale of
    Ghosts; Who Stole the Wizard of
    Oz?*

Narbut, Constable *(Harry),* 57
Narwin, Margaret *(Truth),* 82–88
Nesbit, Edith, *Treasure Seekers,* xiii
Nettie *(Barn),* 135, 137–39
Nevill *(Shadrach),* 123–25, 127
New York City, xv, 4 , 70–74, 168–69
Newbery Award, 13, 88, 109
Newt *(Snail),* 7
Night Journeys, xvi, 36, 37–40, 41, 43,
    63; sequel (see *Encounter at
    Easton)*
No More Magic, xvi, 24, 30–24, 60,
    117, 129
Noel *(Name),* 93
Nothing but the Truth, xvii, 33, 70,
    79–88, 135, 158, 160, 163, 167
nuclear family, 129–30, 144

O'Brien Robert C., *Mrs. Frisby and
    the Rats of NIMH,* 17
Ocax, Mr. *(Poppy),* 17–21
O'Connell, Annie *(Escape),* 140–41,
    147
O'Connell, Gregory *(Escape),* 140
O'Connell, Maura *(Escape),* 140–43,
    145, 147–48
O'Connell, Patrick *(Escape),* 140–43,
    145–48
O'Connell, Timothy *(Escape),* 141
O'Dell, Scott, 35, 50
Orchard Books, 162
Oregon Trail, 135
Oxnard, Sheriff *(Punch),* 132, 134

parents: absent, 30, 90; as authority,
    118; divorced, 123
parody, xvi, 36, 52. *See also* farce;
    mimicry; satire; spoof
Paulson, Gary, 160
Peggy *(Tom),* 28

206 *Index*

The Authors

Susan P. Bloom is an assistant professor and director of the Center for the Study of Children's Literature at Simmons College in Boston. A former high school English teacher at both public and private secondary schools, she has committed her academic career to strengthening the connection between books and young readers. As an instructor of freshman writing and of a survey course in children's literature, Ms. Bloom emphasized to her students the link between reading and writing. Currently she teaches graduate courses in children's literature, which range from the picture book to the young adult novel. In 1991 Ms. Bloom co-authored *Presenting Zibby Oneal* with Cathryn M. Mercier. Ms. Bloom chaired the 1995 *Boston Globe-Horn Book* Award committee and served as a member of the 1997 Newbery Committee.

Cathryn M. Mercier is an assistant professor and associate director of the Center for the Study of Children's Literature at Simmons College. Her frequent contributions to children's literature include reviews for *Five Owls* and *Horn Book Magazine* and biocritical essays in *Twentieth Century Writers for Children, Innocence and Experience: Essays and Conversations in Children's Literature,* and *Writers of Multicultural Fiction for Young Adults.* She has also written analytical essays in *Evaluating Children's Books: A Critical Look* and *Children's Books and Their Creators.* Ms. Mercier has spoken on critical theory in children's literature at national conferences. She chaired the *Boston Globe-Horn Book* Award committee, served on the Caldecott Award committee, and judged the first New Hampshire Writers' Project Awards in literature for children and young adults.

The Editor

Patricia J. Campbell is an author and critic specializing in books for young adults. She has taught adolescent literature at UCLA and is the former Assistant Coordinator of Young Adult Services for Los Angeles Public Library. Her literary criticism has been published in the *New York Times Book Review* and many other journals. From 1978 to 1988 her column, "The YA Perplex," a monthly review of young adult books, appeared in the Wilson Library Bulletin. She now writes a column on controversial issues in adolescent literature for *Horn Book* magazine. Campbell is the author of five books, among them *Presenting Robert Cormier,* the first volume in the Twayne Young Adult Author Series. In 1989 she was the recipient of the American Library Association Grolier Award for distinguished achievement with young people and books. A native of Los Angeles, Campbell now lives on an avocado ranch near San Diego, where she and her husband, David Shore, write and publish books on overseas motorhome travel and she heads a literary agency specializing in young adult fiction.